DESCARTES'S RULES FOR THE DIRECTION OF THE MIND

DESCARTES'S RULES
FOR THE
DIRECTION OF THE MIND

by the late
HAROLD H. JOACHIM

Formerly Wykeham Professor of Logic
In the University of Oxford

Reconstructed from Notes
taken by his Pupils

Edited by Errol E. Harris
Foreword by Sir David Ross

GREENWOOD PRESS, PUBLISHERS
WESTPORT, CONNECTICUT

Library of Congress Cataloging in Publication Data

Joachim, Harold Henry, 1868-1938.
  Descartes's Rules for the direction of the mind.

  Reprint of the 1957 ed. published by Allen & Unwin,
London.
  Includes bibliographical references and index.
  1. Descartes, René, 1596-1650. Regulae ad
directionem ingenii. 2. Reasoning. 3. Logic, Symbolic
and mathematical. 4. Science--Methodology. I. Harris,
Errol E. II. Title.
[B1868.R43J6 1979]   160   79-9958
ISBN 0-313-21263-5

First published in 1957 by George Allen & Unwin Ltd.,
London.

Reprinted with the permission of Nina Joachim.

Reprinted in 1979 by Greenwood Press, Inc.
51 Riverside Avenue, Westport, CT 06880

Printed in the United States of America

10 9 8 7 6 5 4 3 2 1

EDITOR'S PREFACE

★

During the early 1930's, Harold H. Joachim, as Wykeham Professor of Logic at Oxford, delivered the *Logical Studies* as a course of lectures extending over two terms of the academic year, and in the third term he delivered a set of lectures on the *Regulae* of Descartes. The *Logical Studies*, have long since been published, but the manuscript of the Descartes lectures was lost, and there is reason to believe that it was accidentally destroyed with certain domestic papers of no philosophical importance. With the extinction of all hope of finding the original manuscript it seems fitting that, rather than submit to the complete loss of this work to the world of scholarship, an attempt should be made to reconstruct it from the notes taken by some of those who heard the lectures. Two sets of notes (all, so far as I can ascertain, that are available) have been used for this purpose: those of Mr. John Austin, now White's Professor of Moral Philosophy at Oxford, and my own. Let me at once record my gratitude to Professor Austin for the use he has allowed me of his excellent set of notes. It was my own endeavour as a student to get down, so far as was physically possible, every word of Joachim's lectures, but Professor Austin, by adopting a more telegraphic style, succeeded in recording even more of the substance and detail of the lectures than I had.

In attempting to reconstruct what Joachim had actually written, I have tried not to omit anything of the least importance which is contained in either set of notes. Where they were verbally identical little difficulty presented itself and it seemed safe to presume that here one had very nearly, if not exactly, what the lecturer had said. Where the notes differed verbally but not in sense, I have adopted, whichever rendering seemed to me to express better the thought of the author as I remember it. If in this respect there was little to choose between the two versions, I have adopted the one which (with least adjustment or modification) would read better. But both versions are no more than students' notes, taken in lectures and written under pressure of time, and it has been necessary throughout to make minor corrections and to supply omissions, both in order to produce a continuous prose style and in order to clarify the meaning. That these corrections and intercalations are even near to what Joachim wrote or would have written (had he lived to revise the work) there is, of course, no means of knowing, but I have constantly kept in mind the sort of thing that I remember he used to say as well as what he has written elsewhere.

If Joachim had lived it is almost certain that he would not have permitted the publication of his own notes before he had carefully revised them more than once. He would probably have corrected and modified them or even rewritten them either wholly or in part. He would presumably have written a conclusion to avoid the abruptness with which these lectures end. In short, the publication of the present version is to be tolerated only as a lesser evil than the total loss of the thought and work on this subject of one of the most erudite and careful scholars of the last generation.

It is, further, regrettable that the appearance of this work of Joachim's should have been so long delayed. But it was necessary to make sure that no original, nor any better and more authentic version, was ever likely to become available before resorting to the very inferior substitute of students' notes. In the meantime further research has been done on the subject of Descartes's method and, in particular on the *Regulæ*. New editions (e.g. by Leroy and Gouhier) have appeared and a number of works in French, besides Dr. L. J. Beck's admirable book in English. The reader will have to bear in mind that Joachim's lectures predate all these, and that much which he wrote in 1930 (or thereabouts) he would undoubtedly have reconsidered had he lived to read and know of this more recent work. But the extent to which he would have modified his own writing cannot be known. I have, therefore, made no attempt to edit the lectures in the light of later research. It is not impossible that scholars writing after Joachim would themselves have been influenced by his thought had it been published in time. It seems to me that, in the circumstances, it is important to make this little work available in the best form possible without more ado, as something of lasting value to philosophers in general and to Cartesian scholars in particular. It is not for me (or, as I see it, for even more competent persons) to correct what Joachim wrote in the light of later scholarship as it cannot be known whether, to what extent, or in what way, he would have done so himself.

There is one further consideration. The contemporary idiom in Anglo-Saxon philosophy is so utterly different from that in which Joachim wrote and thought only twenty years ago, that many students may question the value of this publication. That the work is at least of historical interest, both in itself and as a contribution to the history of philosophy no genuine scholar will deny. But it is of even greater value than that in as much as it is a contribution (far greater than its physical size suggests) to a kind of philosophy which, if it is at present not so widely practised, nevertheless, has in it much sound substance and significance, and one which may well return to fashion in the not far distant future. There are signs that, for all their vigour, contemporary empiricisms have reached the limit of profitable development. Even professional philosophers may shortly be forced to look elsewhere for fruitful means of advance, if only by the pressure exerted upon them by the progress of the natural sciences, the direction of which seems to point to a philosophy very different from that now current, or by the demand for a re-interpretation of human experience, which the inescapable course of international politics makes upon them.

It remains only for me gratefully to acknowledge the assistance of the University of the Witwatersrand whose subvention has made the publication of this book possible.

ERROL E. HARRIS

The University of the Witwatersrand
Johannesburg 1955

CONTENTS

★

FOREWORD

★

I have gladly accepted Professor Harris's invitation to me
to write a brief introduction to his edition of Professor
Joachim's lectures on Descartes's *Rules for the Direction
of the Mind*. I had the good fortune of knowing Professor
Joachim for the last forty years of his life. His philosophical views have been admirably described and discussed in
Joseph's memoir of him in vol. 24 of the *Proceedings of
the British Academy*, and any who wish to see a sym-
pathetic and yet critical account of them cannot do better
than read that memoir. My own attitude towards
Joachim's philosophy is not unlike that of Mr. Joseph. I
cannot accept Joachim's coherence theory of truth. But I
greatly admire its scholarship and exactness of his exposition, whether the philosopher he was concentrating on
was Aristotle or Descartes or Spinoza; in each of those
fields of study, he was a master. In the interpretation of
Aristotle the student's first task is to discover what
Aristotle actually wrote, and that involves the careful
study of the manuscript tradition and of the ancient com-
mentators, and the establishment of a correct text, in
which even the punctuation is a matter of importance.
Joachim's scholarship and skill in all this I was able to
observe at the weekly meetings of the Oxford Aristotelian
Society from 1900-1914, and in reading his recently
published commentary on the *Nicomachean Ethics*.

His work on Descartes and on Spinoza exhibits the same
qualities of scholarship and of philosophical acumen. His
book on Spinoza is the best study in the English language

at any rate of this great philosopher. Professor Harris has been able to reconstruct, from his own notes and those of other pupils, Joachim's lectures on Descartes, the original manuscript of which was unfortunately lost. In this reconstruction some of the nuances of his exposition will no doubt have been lost, but enough remains to make Professor Harris's edition a most valuable contribution to the study of Descartes.

Mr. T. S. Eliot, who was Joachim's pupil at Merton College, has borne testimony to the close but luminous style (to quote the words of the present Warden of Merton) of his writing; and any of his philosophical colleagues at Oxford who are still alive would bear testimony to the clarity and firmness (combined with exquisite courtsey) with which he would expound his views or criticise those of others. Professor Harris's book will revive in our minds the impression which Joachim made in our oral discussions.

W. D. Ross.

INTRODUCTION

★

Charles Adam suggests that the *Regulae ad Directionem Ingenii*, the unfinished dialogue, *La Recherche de la
Verité par la Lumiere Naturelle*, and *Le Monde* are related to *Discours de la Méthode*, *Meditationes* and
Principia Philosophiae as the first crude sketch for a
finished masterpiece.[1] This view is fully confirmed by
comparison of the *Regulae* with the *Discours*.

The *Discours* was first published in 1637 (when
Descartes was 41 years old) as the exposition of the
general principles of the Cartesian method. It is
masterly in conception and exposition, as well as in
its lucidity and coherence. The *Regulae*, in contrast,
was written probably in the winter of 1628-9, or even
earlier, and is unfinished[2] and in many ways imperfect.
The work is immature and was probably left unfinished because of its defects. Descartes is still, in some
respects, feeling his way. His exposition is often confused and rambling and is sometimes inconsistent. He
is more dogmatic than in the later works, in which
some of the doctrines here stated are rejected or
modified. The work is also immature in form. For

---

[1] Cp. Adam & Tannery, X, pp. 530-2 and XII, pp. 146ff.
[2] There were to have been 36 rules (cf. *Reg.* xii), but only 21 exist,
and the last three lack explanatory expositions.

example, Rule xi[1] merely repeats Rule vi[2] in a compressed form; the long autobiographical passage at the end of the exposition of Rule iv[3] seems to have been added as an afterthought and is ill-fitting in that place, and Rule viii combines, without reconciliation, a rough draft with a more finished but incompatible version.

Owing to these defects, most editors pass over the *Regulae* with brief notice, and the accepted and authoritative account of Descartes's method is based on the *Discours*. But a detailed study of the *Regulae* is instructive as well as interesting, if for no other reason than that it constitutes the first material for the examination of the Cartesian conception of *vera mathesis*. Though nothing emerges in the *Regulae* which is irreconcilable with the traditional exposition of the method, yet it presents difficulties which do not appear in the *Discours*, and so provides a fuller understanding of Descartes's teaching.

HISTORY OF THE MSS[4]

Descartes died at Stockholm on the 11th February, 1650. Two inventories of his papers were made, one at Stockholm, on the 14th of February, of papers he had brought into Sweden, and the second at Leyden, on the 4th of March, of papers left in Holland. M. Jean de Raey, a Professor at Leyden and friend of Descartes, testifies that these were few and of small importance

[1] A. and T., X, pp. 409-410.
[2] Ibid., pp. 384-7.
[3] Ibid., pp. 374-9.
[4] Cp. A. & T., X, pp. 1-14, 351-7, 486-8.

as Descartes took the best with him to Sweden.[1] Of the earlier inventory, made 3 days after Descartes's death, two manuscript copies survive.[2] There are 23 rubrics and the *Regulae* is mentioned under Rubric F: *'Neuf cahiers reliez ensemble, contenans partie d'un traité des regles utiles et claires pour la direction de l'Esprit en la recherche de la Verité'.*[3]

All (except domestic papers) that were contained in this inventory were entrusted to M. Chanut, French ambassador to Queen Christina of Sweden; he conveyed them to Paris, and, being too busy himself to publish any of the manuscripts, entrusted all or most of them to his brother-in-law Clerselier[4] who was also a friend of Descartes.

Clerselier published three volumes of letters in 1657, 1659 and 1667. He also published, in one volume, a treatise on Man (*L'homme*), in 1664, and in the second edition (1677) added '*Le Monde (ou Traité de la Lumiere).* In a preface to Vol. III of the letters, Clerselier says that there are still more than enough MSS. to make another volume of fragments and offers them to anyone who is willing to edit them. Nobody accepted the offer and Clerselier died in 1684 leaving them unpublished. He passed the MSS. on to the Abbé Jean Baptiste Legrand who set out admirably to produce a complete edition of all Descartes's posthumous works, but he died in 1704 before the edition was finished, leaving its completion to Marmion. But he too died,

---

[1] A. & T., V, p. 410.
[2] A. & T., X, pp. 5-12.
[3] Ibid. p. 9.
[4] Vide ibid., p. 13.

in 1705. There does exist in Paris a richly annotated copy of Clerselier's three volumes with marginal notes, additions and corrections in the hand of Legrand, of Marmion and of Baillet (Descartes's biographer).

After Marmion's death the papers reverted to Legrand's mother and it is not known what became of them thereafter. The MS. of the *Regulae* has thus vanished, but a number of people saw and used it: (i) The second edition of the Port Royal Logic (Arnaud and Nicole, 1664[1]) contains a long extract from Rules xiii and xiv translated into French. This the editors owed to Clerselier who lent them the MS.[2] (ii) Nicolas Poisson in his *Remarques sur la Méthode de M. Descartes* (1670) says that he saw the MS.[3] (iii) Perhaps Clerselier also showed it to Malebranche, who himself published a work in 1674-5 under the same title as *Le Recherche de la Verité*. (iv) Baillet, in his Life of Descartes (1691) quotes the *Regulae* freely and uses them in many places. He says Legrand lent him the MS.[4] (v) A note discovered at Hanover in Leibniz's handwriting says that with Tschirnhaus he visited Clerselier, who showed them both certain MSS of Descartes including *Le Recherche de la Verité* and '22 rules explained and illustrated'.[5]

At least two MS. copies of the *Regulae* were made in Holland. One was bought by Leibniz in September 1670 from Dr. Schuller for the Royal Library at Hanover, where it now remains. It is an inferior version

---

[1] The first edn. appeared in 1662.
[2] Vide A. & T., X, p. 352.
[3] Ibid.
[4] Cp. ibid.
[5] Cp. ibid. pp. 208-9.

with many omissions and mistakes. Leibniz (not at the time knowing Descartes's handwriting) says that it is in the author's own hand, but this is not the case. The other copy is much better and probably belonged to Jean de Raey. It was used for the Flemish translation of 1684 by Glazemaker and served, no doubt, as the original for the Amsterdam edition of *Opuscula Postuma* of 1701. The version given by Adam and Tannery is based primarily on this, which they refer to as 'A', correcting it at times from the Hanover MS. (for which the reference is H).

DATE OF COMPOSITION[1]

Adam suggests the winter of 1628-9 as the time when Descartes wrote the Regulae. Between 1629 and 1650 Descartes's letters give much information about his writings but say nothing of the *Regulae*. He is known to have spent the years 1618-25 travelling and soldiering; from 1625 to 1628 he stayed in Paris, which he found distracting and so unfavourable to study that he decided to go into retirement and, before he repaired to Holland 'to seek solitude'[2] (as we learn from one of his letters), he spent the winter in the country in France 'where he made his apprenticeship.'[3] It seems from the context, however, that this means little more than that he accustomed himself to solitude at this time. Adam, nevertheless, suggests that it was then that the *Regulae* was written; but Gilson believes that it can be put much earlier and goes back to the

[1] Cp. A. & T., X. pp. 486-8.
[2] A. & T., X, p. 487.
[3] A. & T., V, p. 558.

time when Descartes was engaged on his first work, which was to have been called, *Studium Bonae Mentis*.

THE ORIGINAL TITLE

In the A version the title given is '*Regulae ad Directionem Ingenii*' : in the H. Version '*Regulae ad Inquirendam Veritatem*'. Baillet combines these and Leibniz refers to 'The Search after Truth'. Perhaps the original MS. had both, either as alternatives or combined as Baillet has them.

CHAPTER I

THE POWER OF KNOWING

★

RULE I : The first of Descartes's rules is not quite as simple and obvious as it appears. The ultimate aim of study should be to guide the mind so that it can pass solid and true judgements on all that comes before it.

In the exposition Descartes begins by contrasting art or craft with science or speculative knowledge. Art involves the acquisition of some special bodily skill, so no one person can be master of all the arts. Science needs no bodily training, no development of the body or any part of it. The power of knowing is a purely spiritual power, single, self-identical and absolute (as opposed to bodily skills). It retains its single character in every field. One may call it 'human or universal wisdom', or 'good sense' (*bona mens*), or the 'natural light' of reason. It must be regarded as a spiritual light which is no more modified by the diversity of the objects it illuminates than is sunlight by the things on which it shines. It is an intellectual vision, a single, natural power of discriminating the true from the false.

The knowledge of a science (unlike a craft) does not destroy, but increases the power to learn others.

All sciences are interconnected, so that it is easier to learn all together than each in isolation. They are simply the universal wisdom variously applied. If we want to search for the truth about things, therefore, we must make it our object to increase the natural light of reason in ourselves. The same *vis cognoscens* is at work throughout, and we must make it our whole aim to increase this perfectly general power. Indeed there are legitimate results to be had from the study of the special sciences (e.g. the cure of disease and the supreme pleasure of the vision of new truth); but these special rewards are irrelevant and to aim primarily at them would be to endanger the success of our main enterprise. We must think only of cultivating the natural light.

The last sentence of the exposition of Rule 1^1 *seems* to insist on the supremacy of the practical end, but full and careful study shows that Descartes's real purpose was to demonstrate the identity of reason in speculation and in practice. The same *bona mens* is the condition both for the discovery of truth and for the conduct of life. Intelligent insight must precede judgement. All judgement whether speculative or practical is for Descartes (or so at least he says later) an act of will—assent to or dissent from an idea —which soon goes beyond all knowledge by mere observation. Thus it is better to pursue studies with a general aim than to work at special problems.

We must attend to two matters in this exposition: (i) The severance of the power of knowing from all corporeal functions and (ii) its singleness. (i) The first

[1] A. & T., X, p. 361.

is only lightly touched on here. In the exposition of Rule xii,[1] however, he supplements this and sketches in detail his view of the knowing subject, the doctrine underlying which seems to be the same as that elaborated in the *Meditationes* and the *Principia Philosophiae* (I, § viii, et. seq). In Rule xii, however, he does not attempt to explain what the mind or the body is or how the body is informed by mind, but is content to put forward his theory of the knowing subject merely as an hypothesis, which may be summarized as follows:—

There are in the knowing subject four faculties: sense, imagination, memory and intellect, of which only the last can perceive truth, the other three playing subsidiary parts. What in us knows is purely spiritual, not a bodily function nor conditioned by the body. This power may cooperate with and apply itself to sense, imagination and memory: it may attend to them; but the activity of knowing is attributed to a single spiritual power only—the *vis cognoscens*, by which in the true sense, (*proprie*) we know. When its activity is pure, then we are said *intellegere*, and the faculty concerned is intelligence. It is in consequence of this purely spiritual power alone that there is any knowledge (properly so-called) in human experience.

Here, then, Descartes characterizes sense, imagination and memory purely as the properties of bodily functions and changes. It is only as such that there is anything distinctive about them. True, these bodily functions and changes are connected with the activity of the spiritual faculty, which may attend to, and so make use of, them; but, strictly, sense, imagination

[1] Ibid., pp. 411-418.

21

and memory are not different forms or grades of knowing. The knowing is always the same throughout and is due to a single spiritual principle—a common, abstractly identical element in them all—the activity of the self-conscious or rational soul. To characterize the three subsidiary faculties, therefore, we must attend to what is peculiar to them and leave the intellect out.

So considered, in their proper nature, they are corporeal organs, with definite location and extension. The action of other parts of the body produces in them, by the ordinary laws of extension and motion, physical changes: i.e. sensations, images, etc.[1] Descartes says, therefore, that we must regard sensation as a change in which we are passive. Our external parts sensate, strictly, only by being acted upon. No doubt, when we apply our peripheral sense organs to an object, it is an action which we initiate, but sensating itself is a purely physical change in the organ. It is a change of shape or form (*idea*) produced by the object on the surface of the organ, as real as the change of shape on the surface of wax produced by a signet. This change of shape is instantaneously communicated to the central part of the body, which Descartes (with the Schoolmen) calls *sensus communis*, the Common Sense, but this communication involves no material transference.[2] In principle it is the same as the movement of the pen as it writes: that of the pen-point being simultaneous with that of all parts of the pen and of the pen as a whole.

The peripheral organ of sense communicates to the

[1] Cp. A. & T, X, pp. 412-13.
[2] Vide ibid., p. 414.

central organ (*sensus communis*) changes of shape or form (*figura vel idea*) and common sense stamps these on the *phantasia* or imagination—just as a signet stamps shapes in the wax (and this, be it noted, is no mere analogy but a literal comparison). The *phantasia* is a real part of the body (*vera pars corporis*), which possesses a determinate size and is situated in the brain. It can assume different shapes in its several portions, so that it can hold and retain a plurality of distinct shapes (or ideas). So regarded it is memory.

The way in which the spiritual power (*intellectus*) cooperates with these bodily organs is not, according to Descartes's account,[1] very clear. He says that either it receives a shape simultaneously from common sense and the imagination, or attends or applies itself to shapes preserved in the memory, or forms new shapes in the imagination. The *vis cognoscens* sometimes suffers and sometimes acts; is sometimes the signet and sometimes the wax, but here the simile *is* mere analogy. There is nothing in physical things in the least like the power of knowing.

Hence the *phantasia* is a genuine part of the body and *phantasmata* are bodily changes in it. Descartes insists that these alterations involve no material transference from the external thing to the sense-organ (e.g. physical particles), or from the sense-organ to the *sensus communis* and from it to the phantasia. Clearly he wishes to free himself from the confused conceptions of curious entities (like *species intentionales*) and the use made of them by the theory of knowledge taught at the Jesuit School of La Fléche in which he

---

[1] Ibid., pp. 415-16,

had been brought up.[1] He is also anxious to emphasize the contrast between the extended body and the purely spiritual intelligence of mind. Yet he does still retain material intermediaries between the mind which knows and the object perceived: forms or shapes in imagination. And these *phantasmata* are genuinely corporeal; yet they are somehow properties, or qualities, not attached to any bodies or tied to any corporeal substance. They are shapes or changes which travel without being attached to any material particles (cp. the modern notion of 'waves').

This strange and obscure doctrine of the bodily *phantasia* is always in the background of the *Regulae*.

(ii) The Singleness of the *vis cognoscens*.

Why does Descartes emphasize the singleness of the *vis cognoscens*? Is it in order to suggest the mutual dependence of all truths and the unity of all sciences? His language here and later suggests that the power of knowing is single in an abstract (or monotonous) sense. All details in any region of the knowable and the different regions of knowledge are one merely in the sense that they are all perceived by the one, single, undifferentiated power—all bathed in the single, undifferentiated spiritual light. This seems to imply that the mutual interdependence of truths in a science leaves the truths themselves unaffected. By a

---

[1] Cp. Gilson. *La Philosophie de Saint Bonaventure*, pp. 146 ff., on the subject of phantasmata and the part they play in the theories of Aquinas and the Schoolmen; esp. pp. 158 ff. on *species intentionales* in the *Summa Philosophica* of Brother Eustace of St. Paul, a textbook which Descartes himself studied at school. In a letter written in 1640 (A & T, III, p. 185) he says that he remembers some of it.

24

single science Descartes could mean an aggregate of unit truths in mutual isolation, not a whole system of truth. Similarly, if this is what he intends, the unity of the sciences seems only to mean that these collections or complexes of unit truths may themselves be gathered into an aggregate of aggregates. We do not yet, however, know properly how Descartes does understand this singleness of the *vis cognoscens* or unity of the sciences.

RULES II AND III

RULE II: We ought to study exclusively subjects which our mind seems competent to know with a certainty beyond all doubt.
RULE III: In whatever subject we thus propose we must enquire not what others believe but only what can be clearly perceived or with certainty inferred, these being the only ways in which genuine knowledge can be acquired.

In the exposition of these two rules, there are two main points to which we must attend: (i) Descartes's attitude to Mathematics and (ii) his conception of the power of knowing as comprising both *intuitus* and *deductio*—both insight and illation.

The first will involve an account of Descartes's conception of *mathesis vera* (*or universalis*) and this may be postponed until we come to discuss Rule iv. But we may consider here why Descartes regarded mathematical science as the most perfect form of science, and what is its special propaedeutic power?[1]

---

[1] Cp. *Discours*, A. & T., VI, pp. 19-22.

Two things impressed Descartes in the contemporary 'vulgar' arithmetic and geometry: (i) its infallible certainty and self-evidence[1]—about any matter there is one truth only, so that a child who has done an addition sum has found out all that the mind of man could discover relative to it; (ii) the way in which this self-evidence expands to cover whole intricate problems. We frequently find a solution to a most complex problem by long trains of reasoning in which each step is very simple yet quite infallible, and the steps are so ordered that we can go easily from one to another. Descartes was firmly convinced that knowledge, in the only proper sense (*scientia*) is certain, evident, indubitable and infallible in sharp contrast with conjecture and opinion, however probable, or thinking which is susceptible of doubt in however small degree.

Nor must knowledge be confused with memory. To remember is not, *qua* memory, the same thing as to know; not even the memory of demonstrations. We might remember all Euclid without knowing it: for knowledge is *spiritual insight* into the matters which may be marshalled by memory.

On this view no science (except, perhaps, arithmetic and geometry) will stand the test, and only mathematics will survive this definition of knowledge. All other sciences give conclusions which are doubtful, or even errors; mathematics alone contains truth and nothing but truth, free from falsity and doubt. How can this be? Descartes early asked himself what gives absolute certainty to this science: why the power of knowing has only attained perfect realization here. And he concluded that it was due to the extreme purity and sim-

[1] Ibid., p. 21.

plicity of the objects with which the geometer and the arithmetician are concerned. They presuppose nothing dependent on experience, nothing requiring confirmation by experiment or observation. The data are entirely simple, abstract and precise; and these sciences consist in logical expansion of such data, rationally deducing consequences from them.

Now Descartes maintains that the power of knowing is neither more nor less than (i) the power of seeing simple data—spiritual insight (*intuitus*) and (ii) the power of moving uninterruptedly from simple to simple—the power of illation (*illatio*). This continuous movement is such that all the links and every connexion are seen by the mind with the same immediate and infallible insight as that with which it intuits the data themselves.

In arithmetic and geometry we have the only satisfactory realization of knowledge, precisely because they contain simple data such as it is the very nature of the intellect to perceive, and everything else is merely the formation of chains in which simple is linked to simple—just such necessary expansion and connexion of data as it is the nature and function of the intellect, in its illative movement, to effect.

So the essence of Descartes's method is (i) to admit no step which is not self-evident and (ii) in moving from step to step, to follow the inevitable logical order. This was the result of reflection upon the actual procedure of geometry and arithmetic. He thought that these conditions would be fulfilled so long as the intellect worked according to its own proper nature. But he came immediately to the realization of defects in the existing mathematical sciences and thought a new universal mathematics to be necessary. This brought him to the conception of a possible universal and flawless mathematics. Tested by the two indispensable requirements, even Arithmetic and Geometry, as then taught, fell short of what he thought a perfect science ought to be. This explains the guarded language at the end of the exposition of Rule ii:[1] that we should not study Geometry and Arithmetic alone, except for disciplinary purposes (and even they would be better served by universal mathematics[2]). This rule then asserts only that we must not study anything which is not as certain as mathematics.

Descartes's account of the Intellect

(1) *Intuitus*. Descartes speaks at times as if *intuitus* and *deductio* were two quite distinct powers, faculties, or activities of the mind. It is, however, unlikely that he ever held so crude a view, or, if he did, he soon abandoned it. Nevertheless, he begins by characterizing *intuitus* as a distinct act or function of mind directed upon a distinct and special kind of object. It is intellectual 'seeing' and has a certainty peculiar to itself, which must not be confused with the vividness of sense-perception or imagination.[3]

As an act of mind *intuitus* is a function of the intellect expressing its own nature. Sometimes what we intuit is a material or corporeal thing, or a relation between such things. In this case, imagination will help, if we visualize the bodies; or sensation may

[1] A. & T., X, p. 366.
[2] Vide Rule IV.
[3] Cp. *Reg.* III.

help, if imagination is directed upon the shapes in the *sensus communis*. Still, intellectual seeing must be clearly distinguished from sensation and imagination, and its certainty must be clearly distinguished from mere imaginative (or sensational) assurance. So Descartes begins by explaining what he does not mean by *intuitus*.

The intellectual certainty with which I see the mutual implication of self-consciousness and existence is immediate, like sense-perception; but, in the case of sense-perception, my assurance fluctuates. Sensation flickers and varies according to the illumination, or the state of my eyesight, or similar changing conditions. But the certainty of intellectual insight is steady, constant and absolute. To see a truth—that x implies y—is to see it absolutely and timelessly, once for all and unvaryingly.

The danger of confusing *intuitus* with *imaginatio* depends on the fact that, in both, two or more elements are connected and the pictured union may be more vivid than the conceived 'cohesion'. But we must not confuse 'co-picturable' with 'co-thinkable' (conceivable) for these are not the same. Nor is 'unpicturable' the same as inconceivable.

The text, however, is obscure. In Rule iii[1] he writes *'Per intuitum intelligo non fluctuantem sensuum fidem, vel male componentis imaginationis judicium fallax'*. And in Rule xii[2] he seems to imply that ideal elements may be composed in imagination in two quite different ways: (i) as dictated by the intellect and (ii) alogically and arbitrarily, due to the order of

[1] A. & T., X, p. 368.
[2] Ibid., pp. 416 and 421-4.

succession or co-existence originally produced in the peripheral organ of sense. This second kind of combination may be accepted and confirmed by the subject, to whom it may dictate a judgement, which is then likely to be erroneous (*male componentis imaginationis*)—for which imagination *alone* is responsible and which is apt to deceive us. Connexion resulting from mere casual association is doubtful, for, unless controlled by the intellect, imagination often connects and compounds elements which do not really belong together and so should not be connected. Judging this connection to be fact, we are, consequently, in error.

Descartes's mature theory is that judgement involves assent or dissent to a content conceived—and this assent or dissent is an act of will. This theory is hinted at in the last sentence of the exposition of Rule i; but apart from this hint he seems, at this stage, to be working without any special theory and to be merely accepting the traditional scholastic view. In Rule iii, belief is seen to be an obscure topic and is said to be an action, not of the mind but of the will.[1] At this date, therefore, Descartes presumably did not attribute to the will judgements in which we assent to rules we know or certainly apprehend. Likewise, in the exposition of Rule xii,[2] he distinguishes the faculty by which the intellect sees and knows (*intuetur et cognoscit*) from that which judges in affirming and negating, and here the second faculty is not identified with the will.

Having shown what *intuitus* is not, Descartes goes

---

[1] Ibid., p. 370: ' . . . *fides, quaecumque est de obscuris, non ingenii actio sit, sed voluntatis.*'

[2] A. & T., X, p. 420.

on to state what it is.[1] It is a conception, formed by pure and attentive mind, so easy and distinct that no uncertainty remains. It is thus free from doubt, drawing its origin solely from the light of reason, and is more certain, because more simple, than *deductio*, which, however, even in men, is (on certain conditions) infallible.

'Simplicity', here, does not mean that what is apprehended is atomic. Descartes speaks of 'simple natures' (*naturae simplices*), but refers to them also as propositions, and they are, in fact, always couples of terms in immediate logical relation. Each is genuinely simple: the object is apprehended, not discursively but in its entirety; and both the object and the act itself are present together, all at once and without lapse. In the exposition of Rule iii[2] one of the characteristics by which *intuitus* is opposed to *deductio* is *praesens evidentia*. This is essential to *intuitus*, but not to *deductio*, which can borrow its certainty from memory. In the expositions of Rules xi and xii, the same point is brought out from the side of the object. In the first[3] it is stated that a proposition must be apprehended (i) clearly and distinctly and (ii) all at once, not successively. And in the second[4] we are told that we must be in error if, in regard to a simple nature, we judge that we know it in part only. It is either wholly present and completely revealed or not at all; either it gives us the absolute and entire truth or no intellectual insight at all.

[1] Ibid., p. 368.
[2] Ibid., p. 370.
[3] Ibid., p. 407.
[4] Ibid., p. 420.

The origin of the whole doctrine is obviously Aristotelian. *Intuitus* is the same as νόησις, 'simple natures' are τὰ ἁπλᾶ or τὰ ἀσύνθετα, and the truth of *intuitus* is, like the truth of νόησις[1] opposed, not to error, but to blank ignorance.

When Descartes says that the mind must be attentive and perception distinct, and that one of the two necessary conditions is that propositions should be apprehended clearly and distinctly, he is using more or less technical terms. So, in *Principia Philosophiæ* I, § 45,[2] to perceive anything clearly means that what is perceived is present and open to the mind attending to it, just as objects of sight are clear to the eye when they strike it '*satis fortiter et aperte*'. To perceive distinctly means (in addition to perceiving clearly) that one has before one's mind precisely what is relevant, no more and no less.

Therefore, in an act of *intuitus* the intellect alone must be engaged, and must be concentrated upon an object present to it in its single entirety—an object which is openly and manifestly present to it. This single intentness must, moreover, include all that is essential to the object (every relevant element in it) and must include nothing else.

What is it that we see in such an act of *intuitus*? What is the character of the self-evident object of the intellect? Under Rule iii Descartes gives examples as follows: 'Thus anyone can perceive by the mind that he exists, that he is self-conscious, that a triangle is bounded by three lines only . . .'[3] The object of *intuitus*

---

[1] *Metaphysics* Θ, 1051b17 ff.   [2] A. & T., VIII, p. 22.
[3] Ibid, p. 368: '*Ita unusquisque animo potest intuere, se existere, se cogitare, triangulum terminari tribus lineis tantum . . .*'

therefore, is a proposition in which two elements are in immediate but necessary connection as *implicans* and *implicatum*. A immediately and necessarily involves B—an immediate necessary nexus of a couple of elements. The nexus however need not be reciprocal, as Descartes specially tells us that it is not necessary that B should immediately implicate A.[1] He thus speaks of these self-evident data as *propositiones* or *enunciationes*[2] and he quotes, as further examples, '$2+2=4$', '$3+1=4$', '$2+2=3+1$'.[3] Yet he constantly speaks of these self-evident objects of *intuitus* in terms which suggest *concepta*—an 'A' or a 'B' and not a complex 'A implying B'. He speaks of them as *res simplicissimae* and *naturae purae et simplices*.

It is not easy, at first sight, to reconcile such passages with what must be taken as his considered view: that the object is a nexus. There is a very puzzling passage in the exposition of Rule xii,[4] which may be summarized as follows:

We must distinguish what is a single thing, when things are considered *per se*, from what is single when considered from the point of view (or as an object) of our thought. E.g. a shaped body is a single thing when considered '*ex parte rei*', but as an object of our knowledge it is complex—it is compounded of three '*naturae*': body, extension and figure. Though these have never existed apart, they must be conceived sep-

---

[1] Ibid., p. 422.
[2] Ibid., pp. 369, 370; 379; 383.
[3] Ibid., p. 369.
[4] Ibid., pp. 418-425. *Note*: The doctrine is repeated in various passages of Locke's *Essay Concerning the Human Understanding*. Locke lived in Holland from 1683 to 1689.

arately before we can say that they are found together in one thing. In the *Regulae* we are concerned with things *qua* objects of thought. Hence 'a single thing' must mean what is so clearly and distinctly conceived that we cannot divide it: e.g. duration, extension, figure, motion, etc.; i.e. it is a not further analysable object of knowledge and thought. And it must be a genuine element of an object of knowledge, not a mere generality or abstract universal.[1] For instance 'limit' (in 'Figure is the limit of extension'), is more general than 'figure' (for there may also be a limit of duration or motion), but it is not more simple. It is complex, being a conflation from many simple natures, compounded of several different ideas by disregarding their differences. It is applicable to all only equivocally, and not applicable, in any definite sense, to any.

Descartes shows that all such simple objects of thought fall into three classes: purely intellectual, purely material or corporeal, and those which are common to both. By the first he means objects of thought which are intelligible to self-conscious beings or spirits only, and which are known without any image or other corporeal aid (e.g. knowledge, ignorance, doubt, volition, and what these are). The second are known to exist only in bodies, and intellectual insight into them is facilitated by imagination or sensuous presentation (e.g. figure, extension, motion). The third class of objects is common because they are attributable both to material bodies and to spirits indifferently (e.g. existence, duration, unity). We must here include those common notions which are links connecting other simple natures and on the self-

[1] Cp. pp. 418-9.

evidence of which the conclusions of our demonstrations rest (e.g. identity, equality, etc.: two things equal to the same thing are equal to one another). These common objects may be known by inspection of the intellect, pure and alone, or so far as seeing images of material things reveals them to the intellect, The list of simple natures must be extended to include the corresponding negations and privations of such concepts, so far as they are conceived by the mind: e.g. instant (the negation of duration), rest (the privation of motion), nothing (the negation of existence) and so on.

This and similar passages suggest a sharp distinction between *intuitus* and *deductio* (common in philosophy), and the suggestion is confirmed in the next paragraph,[1] where he distinguishes two faculties of intellect, one which sees and knows, and one which judges by affirming and negating. There are certain symbols which form, so to speak, the letters of the alphabet of reality—universals pervading either all things, spiritual and corporeal, or large areas of the real, but, nevertheless, in some sense singular and simple, They are fundamental constituents of all that exists, and they themselves, though they do not (in the same sense) exist, yet they *subsist*. They are in some sense there, confronting the mind, waiting for its recognition which is direct and immediate—a simple act of seeing. This is the only genuine knowledge, the only real and absolutely certain grasp of truth, the indispensable precondition of judgement and reasoning, which by combining and arranging what we intuit gives a more precarious and derivative knowledge.

[1] Ibid., p. 420.

Yet any such interpretation is not only in direct conflict with what Descartes has said under the earlier Rules about simple propositions being the object of *intuitus*, is not only in conflict with what he says about *deductio*, but can hardly stand and does not, on closer examination, really emerge from the passage under Rule xii, especially if we consider Descartes's examples and his manner of expressing himself.

He says that no corporeal idea can be imagined such as to represent to us what doubt, knowledge, etc., really are. It seems, then, to be implied that what we intuitively perceive is 'that knowledge is so and so'. Again, speaking of the second class of simples, he says that they are known to be only in bodies (that duration is attributed to certain bodies, that 'this body is in motion', etc.); and, of the third, that they are attributed indifferently, now to spirits, now to corporeal things (e.g. 'that this mind exists', 'that this body is extended—at rest, etc.'). There seems no room for hesitation if we bear in mind that Descartes adds to the list of simple natures the principles of linkage of our knowledge, the universally accepted laws of thought. What the intellect perceives, then, is quite clearly, at least two elements in one fact, two elements in immediate and necessary cohesion. The whole fact, in necessary combination, *implicans* plus *implicandum* is 'simple' in that it is a minimum of knowledge. Nothing less is knowable at all. We cannot know 'A' nor 'B', nor 'implying' except in a single unitary whole where all three are distinct (no doubt) but inseparable. If we know at all it must be 'A implying B'.

(2) *Deductio*. The first mention of *deductio* is under Rule ii, where it is contrasted with experience (empirical observation), and these (*deductio* and 'experience') are regarded as two alternative ways by which we can arrive at a knowledge of things. Assuming that we begin with a self-evident truth, we may extend our knowledge by rationally following the implications of the *implicans*—the illation of one thing from another. Experience often misleads us, but *deductio* is quite as infallible as *intuitus* itself. We may fail to make a deduction, we may fail to draw out what is logically implied, but no intellect at all rational can mis-infer or mis-think any more than it can mis-perceive. That is why mathematics is free from error; it is no more than the following out of the logical implications of simple, abstract and absolutely certain data. These, if they are perceived at all, must be perceived as they are, and their implications, as logically drawn out, must be infallible. Observation, on the other hand is fallible.

So far *deductio* takes its place alongside *intuitus* as one of the two necessary and only acts of the *vis cognoscens*. It is the very nature of the intellect to perform both of these activities, and thus we achieve knowledge without any deception. To understand is intellectually to perceive or to deduce or both, and intellectually to perceive or deduce is to understand. There is no such thing as false intuition or faulty deduction. So it appears that one of these native functions of the mind assures us of the data and the other guarantees our advance from the data.[1]

It cannot be denied that the interpretation here given is what Descartes intends. More than once in the *Regulae* he asserts the duality of original acts of the intellect and distinguishes intellectual vision from illative or discursive movement, and the perception of simple reals from the linkage or connexion between simple reals. But in spite of this explicit doctrine, there runs through the *Regulae* a more adequate conception of the function of the intellect, though one incompatible with the doctrine expressed. This more adequate doctrine, which first appears under Rule iii (just as Descartes is formulating the above, more crude, theory), is the more important for our present purpose.[2] We need not discuss whether Descartes ever was a whole-hearted believer in the mechanical analysis of the power of knowing into two functions and the corresponding division of the objects of mind into simple natures and the linkages between them. May he not simply have adopted an expository device? If we think that he really believed it, we must suppose that he was later forced beyond it, but that he never became fully conscious of his own advance and

---

[1] In the passage under Rule III (A. & T., X, p. 368): *omnes intellectus nostri actiones, per quas ad rerum cognitionem absque ullo deceptionis metu possimus pervenire: admittunturque tantum duae, intuitus, scilicet et inductio'*—the word 'inductio' is probably an error in the MS., for under Rule IV (ibid., p. 372), Descartes refers again to this passage using the word '*deductio*' (cp. also *Reg. ix Exp.*, ibid., p. 400). The matter, however, is complicated by the fact that what Descartes means by '*enumeratio sive inductio*, is uncertain (cp. below, pp. 49-61).

[2] Cp. p. 25 above.

so fell into verbal self-contradictions. On the assumption that he did not really hold such a view, we must suppose that his contradictions are corrections of what he considers to be an inadequate way of expressing his theory.

Under Rule iii, Descartes proceeds to say: 'But this self-evidence and certainty of intellectual insight is required not only for simple propositions but also for all discursive reasoning. For example, 2 and 2 yield the same sum as 3 and 1, in this case we must perceive not only that 2 and 2 make 4, and 3 and 1 likewise make 4, but also that the conclusion is a necessary consequence of these two propositions'.[1]

Under Rule xi we get the same idea: 'The simple deduction of any one thing from another is effected by means of intellectual insight'.[2] And under Rule xii: '. . . the mind's insight extends to the apprehension of simple propositions, their necessary linkages and everything else which the intellect experiences with precision'.[3] Thus *intuitus* is needed for both linkages and simple natures, and there is no sharp division between the objects of *intuitus* and of *deductio*. The difficulty now is to distinguish *deductio* as an original act or function of the intellect—as a separate mode of knowledge—at all. How is it 'other than' *intuitus*, as is alleged under Rule iii?[4]

[1] A. & T., X, p. 369.   [2] Ibid., p. 407.
[3] Ibid., p. 425: '*Atque perspicuum est, intuitum mentis, tum ad illas omnes extendi, tum ad necessarias illarum inter se connexiones cognoscendas, tum denique ad relinqua omnia quae intellectus praecise, vel in se ipso, vel in phantasia esse experitur*'.
[4] Ibid., pp. 369-70.

In order to bring out Descartes's better view we may begin by giving the answer which he ought to have made; then we shall outline the position to which he seems on the whole to have inclined (apart from waverings and contradictions), pointing out where he explicitly departs from it; and, thirdly, we shall attempt to confirm this interpretation by detailed references.

(a) Descartes ought to have said that two things are always essentially involved in every act of knowing: —(i) a certain illative movement or discursus—an intellectual analysis and synthesis in one—which brings to light distinguishable elements and at the same time points to the logical implication by which each leads to the next—the necessary connections by which they cohere; (ii) a certain unitary apprehension, an immediate, direct perception of the distinguishable elements (as opposed to isolable constituents) as indivisibly constituting a whole.

Beyond this no further distinction of *intuitus* from *deductio* is possible or necessary. In principle both modes are essential and indispensable to any and every act of knowing. And in principle the character of every *cognoscibile* and every *cognitum* must be such as to answer to these two modes of apprehension. Nothing is or can be known unless it is unitary and whole and present before the mind in its wholeness, and unless within this unity there are two or more distinguishables, so that it is discovered to the mind by a discursive movement at once analytic and synthetic. The distinguishables are seen in this *discursus* to be mutually implied, as it moves from one to the other along the line of logical connexion. The *discursus* is constructive of a whole and is so far synthetic, but we must not forget its analytic obverse, or we shall tend to attribute to immediate apprehension alone what requires a *discursus* as well, and to postulate the unitary perception of atomic *cognoscibilia*.

The simplest act of mind is *deductio* and *intuitus* in one. The *minimum cognoscible* is a 'simple nature' which is also a proposition—both *conceptum* and *deductum*: each of these only because and in so far as it is the other. Similarly, the most intricate piece of reasoning, or the most complicated system of demonstration if in it we achieve genuine knowledge, is illative movement and direct intellectual vision in inseparable unity—*conceptum* as well as *deductum* or *demonstratum*. If on the side of the intellect either of these is wanting, then the knowing in question is defective—the knowledge is imperfect and the object incompletely intelligible and only partially understood. Owing to the weakness of the human intellect such maimed and limping efforts are at times accepted as genuine knowledge, and similarly mutilated objects as genuine *cognoscibilia*; and so we are led wrongly to assume, on the one hand, atomic elements which can be apprehended immediately and alone, or, on the other hand, long chains of reasoning which subsist without any real unity or wholeness; and to believe that the mind, in knowing thus piecemeal, knows a genuine object in a genuine manner.

(b) What Descartes actually tends to maintain is a compromise between the above position and a neat but wooden analysis, with a sharp distinction between *intuitus* and *deductio*. (i) There are certain primary basal facts, reals or truths—the letters of the alphabet of reality - knowable and known by the immediate intellectual apprehension of *intuitus* alone. These are at once elementary constituents of reality and the foundations of all knowledge. (ii) At the other extreme there are certain remote consequences of these data connected to them by chains of reasoning effected by illative, discursive activity only. The apprehension here takes the form of construction (or re-construction) of the chain of reasoning, enabling us, not to see, but to infer the consequences from the primary data. (iii) Between these two there is an intermediate region of knowledge, where what is known is both seen immediately (intuitively) and apprehended as demonstrable, or inferentially and necessarily deducible, from ultimate *cognoscibilia*.

Nevertheless, Descartes only maintains this compromise with qualifications. First, some of his statements show that he waveringly recognizes that the apprehension of primary reals and truths involves discursus and, secondly, the absence of immediate perception in long chains of reasoning is sometimes ascribed to an *infirmity* in the human mind.[1] What he says implies the recognition that so far as *intuitus* is absent our knowledge is neither genuine nor perfect.

(c) Let us now consider what Descartes actually says in more detail. (i) First, he states a kind of compromise doctrine: some propositions may be said to be known at times by *intuitus*, or at others by *deductio*, according to different points of view, but first principles are known only by *intuitus* and remote conclusions only by *deductio*.[2] It is only such as can be immediately

[1] Cp. below on 'enumeratio sive inductio', pp. 49ff.
[2] A. & T., X, p. 370.

deduced from first principles to which the compromise doctrine applies. Here the discursus may subserve perception, or perception assist the discursus.[1] Again, he says that many things, though not self-evident, may yet be known with certainty, provided only that they are deduced by a continuous and uninterrupted movement of thought from premises which are certain, and that the thinker perceives clearly each single step. Though we cannot embrace all the links of the chain in one act of perception, we can apprehend the connexion of the last stage with the first, without, in the same act, perceiving each several link, provided that we have seen all the links and their several connexions and remember that each was necessarily connected with its neighbour. So *deductio* is contrasted with *intuitus*, first, as movement or succession, and secondly so far as its certainty does not require the '*praesens evidentia*' required by *intuitus*, but is in a manner borrowed from the memory.[2] The middle region of any science or department of the knowable is, then, from different points of view, the object both of *intuitus* and of *deductio*.

Yet Descartes maintains a sharp distinction between *deductio* and *intuitus*, even where they co-operate. Both may be indispensable for a genuine act of knowledge, yet within that act each remains detachable; each remains what it was when it constituted imperfect knowledge by itself. In fact each always remains itself and what it is in isolation, even when both go together in one piece of knowledge. When Descartes says, or implies, that immediate apprehension and

[1] Cp. ibid., pp. 407-8.
[2] Ibid., p. 370.

43

illation are inseparable and indispensable conditions of any full act of knowledge, he still views them as connected *ab extra* with each other. Each requires the other but is not fused with it. Thus, in order to know that $2+2=3+1$ is a necessary consequence of the fact that $2+2=4$ and $3+1=4$, the intellect must perceive by *intuitus* that $2+2=4$ and $3+1=4$, then it must deduce the equality of $2+2$ and $3+1$, and finally it must (again) perceive that the conclusion is a necessary consequence of the premises.

Descartes always tends to conceive reasoning as a chain of links or sequence of states—a movement of thought along a chain of truths, each link being self-evident and the movement from link to link—or rather the connexion of the second link to the first, *after* the movement has been made—must be self-evident. From this point of view, Descartes's *deductio* is the same as the ideally perfect syllogism or ἀπόδειξις of Aristotle. It is true that he protests against syllogism, but unless he mistakes Aristotle he means by that the traditional subsumptive syllogism of the Schoolmen. With that he will have nothing to do, nor with their 'dialectical' reasoning. But his own *deductio* is, nevertheless, the same as Aristotle's 'complete demonstration'. For the perfect ἀπόδειξις, 'A must be Y', has to resolve the interval between A and Y into a succession of minimal, self-evident steps; 'A must be B; B must be C', etc., so that A will be seen to involve B, C, D, and so on, leaving nowhere any interval without immediate judgement. Thus, between A and Y a distance will have to be traversed which, though completely and exclusively covered by self-evident steps, is itself too great for the connexion between the remote extremes to be self-evident. This is the same as Descartes's doctrine.

(ii) Nevertheless, even the apprehension of a primary truth or self-evident simple nature (as we have already asserted) does involve discursus. This becomes apparent in Descartes's reply to the second set of objections to the *Meditations*.[1] The objectors urge against Descartes that he asserts that nothing can be known with absolute certainty unless and until the existence of God—the perfect, omnipotent and truthful being—is known; yet he claims in the second Meditation, though still as yet uncertain of God's existence, clear, distinct and indubitable knowledge of his own existence; and afterwards asserts that this must be deduced from the knowledge of God's existence. Descartes replies[2] that 'cogito ergo sum' is a *prima quaedam notio* not deduced by syllogistic reasoning, yet at the same time he makes it clear that it is a nexus in which two factors, *implicans* and *implicatum*, are necessarily involved. (He means by '*syllogismus*', here, the bringing under a universal rule of a particular instance—'syllogism' as understood by the Schoolmen, but what Aristotle in the *Posterior Analytics* refuses to recognize as true syllogism and regards only as making explicit what is already implicitly known). Descartes easily shows that my own existence, so far from being deduced from a major premise, is prior to any universal major and I can only arrive at the certain knowledge of it by consciousness of what my own experience implies. Spinoza, in his summary of Descar-

[1] A. & T., VII, pp. 124-5.
[2] Ibid., p. 140.

tes's philosophical principles,[1] follows this statement of Descartes's and rightly lays it down that *'cogito ergo sum'* is not a syllogism; but when Spinoza goes on to summarise the position, saying that *'ego sum cogitans'* is a single proposition equivalent to *'cogito ergo sum'*, he has overshot the mark. For Descartes says[2] that a man learns the universal premise from the fact that he experiences in his own case the impossibility of thinking unless he exists. This experience is said to be a recognition by the simple insight of the mind, which seems very forcibly to emphasize that what the mind intuites is a necessary nexus or implication. Thus *'cogito ergo sum'* is, as Spinoza says, a single, unitary proposition (*unica propositio*). But Descartes himself shows that it includes within itself an illation from one element to another. It is a mediate judgement, a concentrated or telescoped inference. The self-evident fact (*'res per se nota'*) is 'that my thinking necessarily implies my existence'.

We may compare this with what Descartes says in the exposition of Rule xii.[3] He has just been distinguishing three classes of simple natures, all of which[4] (e.g. figure, extension, motion, and the like) are *res per se notae*. But he proceeds to say that they are conjoined or compounded with one another and that this conjunction is either necessary or contingent. It is necessary when one is confusedly implied in the

[1] *Renati des Cartes Principia Philosophiae, more geometrico demonstrata*, I, Prolegomenon (*Opera*, Vol. IV, Van Vloten en Land, pp. 112-3).
[2] Loc. cit.
[3] A. & T., X, p. 421.
[4] vide, p. 420.

notion of the other so that we cannot conceive either properly (if at all) if we try to conceive them as independent of each other: e.g. extension and figure or motion and time. Likewise $4+3=7$ is a necessary composition because the notion of seven must confusedly include those of four and three.

The first part of this passage, in spite of its obvious formal inconsistency, must be treated with all respect because it contains the germ of an important later theory of Descartes. The formal inconsistency is that he says motion, extension, etc., are simple natures *per se notae* out of which all our succeeding knowledge is compounded; yet here motion, duration and figure have become implicated in larger and more concrete concepts, and it is these which are clear and distinct, *per se notae*, and knowledge of these is the necessary precondition to that of the so-called simple natures. This inconsistency, however, is of minor importance What must be noted is that the line of thought here implied would lead to the recognition of two clear and distinct, or self-evident, natures only: *substantia extensa* and *substantia cogitans*—there would be a necessary system of extended *implicantia* and *implicata* and also one of spiritual *implicantia* and *implicata*. Here the Cartesian conception is adumbrated of a physical universe, open to thought as a coherent system of mutually implicated data (motion extension, figure, etc.), and its correlate, a corresponding, self-contained, coherent system of spiritual concepts. There is both external and internal logical coherence, and the physical universe is transparent to intellectual insight because and in so far as thought distinguishes certain characters, and in recognizing them is driven to illate from one to another and see them as elements of a self-integrating whole.

But what are we to make of Descartes's statement about $4+3=7$? We saw, in the explanation of Rule iii,[1] that $2+2=4$ and $3+1=4$ were cited as examples of objects of *intuitus*, and *intuitus* alone. They were facts which our intellect alone could directly see, no other method of cognition being required. We should expect, therefore, that $3+4=7$ would be the same. But here it is called a composition of simple natures, and one which is necessary and not contingent because the conception of 7 involves confusedly 3 and 4. What then are the 'simple natures'?—3 and 4, or 3 +4, or 7? It seems that 3 and 4 could not be simple if 7 is not. Yet the conception of 7 is clearly admitted to include the conceptions of 3 and 4 as well as their addition. It seems that here Descartes, consciously or not, does recognize a movement of thought within and constituting the clear and distinct intellectual vision.

So far as any reasoning remains sheerly discursive, without there being any comprehensive conception, or immediate intuition covering the whole, such reasoning is not itself knowledge but an imperfect substitute for knowledge—a limitation or stunting of knowledge—which the mind accepts only because of its infirmity. This also is implied at times by Descartes's express assertion, but to decide how far he intended it we should have to be clear about the meaning of *enumeratio sive inducio'*, which is very difficult to determine and can be assigned only conjecturally.

[1] Ibid., p. 369.

(3) *Enumeratio sive inductio.*

Descartes holds that every possible subject of inquiry is in principle intelligible—that is, reality as a whole and every department of the real, every one of its parts, is a system of intelligibles necessarily connected in inherent logical order. This logical order of linkages is followed by the intellect in knowing, because and in so far as it is neither more nor less than the order proper to *intuitus* and *deductio. Intuitus* reveals the first link in the chain, and provided we advance from link to link by correct logical illation, never breaking the continuity, then every element of every part of reality, as well as the whole, will, in due course be reached. In principle, then, careful logical analysis will enable us to find the links in any sphere of inquiry, so long as we adopt the proper logical order. Everything *can* be known in this way with the same certainty and by the same means. Nothing is too remote; everything can be reached with the same ease, and the knowledge of one thing is never more obscure than that of another, for all complexity consists in *"rerum per se notarum compositio'* (cp. Rule xii, Expos.).

Reality, as a whole is, accordingly, perfectly intelligible, and so is every group of facts; all are, and are knowable as, self-evident constituents self-evidently inter-connected. That is so, at least in principle and ideally—i.e. it would be so for a mind which had mastered every department of knowledge and expounded or unfolded it all in the correct logical order as a single chain of self-evident truths. Descartes, however, seems, at least from Rule v onwards, to conceive ideally perfect knowledge as a network or system of chains, rather than as a single chain; and, secondly, he regards each link as less complex and more simple than its successor—more complex and less simple than its predecessor. But no human mind is capable of mastering every subject of inquiry and all knowledge, so the sum total of our knowledge could not unroll itself (in fact) in a chain, or system of chains, self-evident in every link.

If we reflect upon man's efforts to systematize his knowledge, we shall notice the following three typical cases:-

(i) A single line of logical implication lies straight ahead of us, straight from what lies immediately before us to the conclusion or solution of our problem. In this most favourable case, the whole problem—the whole segment of the real which is being studied—has resolved itself, bit by bit, into its ultimate self-evident constituents and their logically inevitable and self-evident linkages. The only difficulty here arises from the growing length of the chain. When we try to set out the connexions in the best logical order—to connect all the simples discovered, and arrange them as a continuous inevitable illation, with every pair of simples, from first to last, self-evidently connected—we sometimes get a chain so long that we cannot keep it, all at once and as a whole, within the grasp of our intellectual vision. We shall thus be forced to rely to some extent on our memory, and that is fallible. Strictly speaking we do not genuinely know the connexion of the last element with the first unless we can demonstrate it by an unbroken, continuous movement of clear thought. This is never possible if any one link is lost or misplaced, which is liable to happen when we rely on memory; and so is hardly ever possible.

The remedy for this, described by Descartes in Rule vii, is *enumeratio*: the repeated reviewing of every link in the long chain, and re-thinking of the various proofs. Such practice facilitates and strengthens our powers of illation and brings longer and longer chains within the span of intuition. By this means we may extend our powers of deduction to any length, progressively reducing our reliance on memory. Descartes never suggests that the rôle of mere memory can ever be entirely eliminated in this way, but we can shorten the time required for the illation so that less is left for the memory to do and we seem to see all at once.[1] So we may approach the single instantaneous intuition, and Descartes clearly assumes that our knowledge is the more perfect in the degree to which the discursive movement falls within the span of such a single, immediate intuition.

To achieve complete knowledge of any subject we must survey (*perlustrare*), by a continuous and unbroken movement of thought, all matters which belong to our inquiry, singly and together, in a sufficient and well-ordered enumeration.[2] But what this '*enumeratio*' is he does not tell us precisely, for the

[1] Cf. ibid., p. 388: '. . . *donec a prima ad ultimam tam celeriter transire didicerim, ut fere nullas memoriae partes relinquendo, rem totam simul videar intueri*'.

[2] Ibid., p. 387, *Reg.* vii. Cp. *Discours*, A. & T. VI, p. 19: '. . . *de faire partout des denombremens si entiers, et des reveuës si generales, que je fusse assuré de ne rien omettre*'. Also, p. 550: '*ut tum in quaerendis mediis, tum in difficultatum partibus percurrendis, tam perfecte singula enumerarem et ad omnia circumspicerem, ut nihil a me omitti essem certus*'.

enumeration he goes on to describe[1] has no relevance to the difficulty of the length of the chain (as opposed to the heterogeneity or complexity of the elements). It seems as if what he is advocating is no more than some special rubrics for grouping the details—the special proofs or parts of the chain—in fact, any kind of mechanical device to help the memory.

(ii) But as a rule we are in a far less favourable situation, for even if we are following a single line of direct logical implication from a simple datum, our progress may be barred by the nature of the facts (the obstinacy of nature) or by our own relative ignorance and inability. We are trying to resolve a particular problem of a special science; but, in the first place, in defining and delimiting the several domains of the different sciences, we do not divide reality into really separate, self contained and independent worlds, so the direct line of investigation may cut across the accepted boundary marking off the domain of our special science from those of other sciences. The mathematician, for instance, proceeds along a chain of mathematical reasoning, but he may find further progress arrested by an inescapable barrier, if he comes upon a link which has no successor, or direct *implicatum*, within the domain of mathematics. The connexion would then, of necessity, be obscure to him as a mere mathematician, for the *implicatum* may belong to the domain of physics or optics. And, secondly, even if we could assume that the domain of each science is in fact self-contained and that the facts are linked in a single chain, still we do not know the whole science, but only work at a particular problem.

[1] A. & T., X, p. 388.

Thus it would be very unlikely that the links we know should all be adjacent or neighbouring links in the chain, or that our analysis would unfold all the links in all the parts. Consequently, we should from time to time come upon a link of which the immediate necessary implication is not obvious to us and will not become so until we have learned more.

(iii) But in many of our actual scientific reasonings no single, direct line of implication exists, or the manner of our investigation tends to conceal it if it does. For we often move, not from simple to simple, but from many elements taken together to a simgle consequent. The thread of implication is often twisted out of many strands. We must deduce our consequent from an antecedent in fact composed from a set of co-ordinate links or elements each drawn from a different implicatory sequence.[1] We might have said 'induce', rather than 'deduce', for this process is generally called 'induction'. In such cases advance is obstructed, not only by the growing length of the chain, but also by the complexity and heterogeniety of the data and the intricacy of their interconnection. Here, according to Descartes, *enumeratio* is essential as an auxiliary of the deductive process. Indeed he is so impressed by its importance, that at times he speaks of it as though it were an independent method of proof and at others as if it were the only method of proof, as opposed to direct intellectual insight.

Now '*enumeratio sive inductio*' is said to be illation or inference derived and composed from many disconnected things ('*ex multis et disjunctis rebus collec-*

[1] Cp. A. & T., X, p. 429, ll. 19-27.

ta').[1] In a passage describing the same logical procedure, he speaks of 'proving by enumeration' and 'a conclusion drawn by induction'.[2] Yet in at least two other passages he treats of '*enumeratio*' as the only form of *deductio* genuinely distinct from[3] and in no way reducible to *intuitus*.[4] Here Descartes says: 'This is an opportunity to explain more clearly what was earlier said about intellectual insight: since in one place we contrasted it with deduction and in another with enumeration only ...' (i.e. not with deduction in general but with enumeration in particular). Simple deduction of one thing from another takes place through intuition (*per intuitum*), and for this two conditions must be satisfied: The proposition must be apprehended (a) clearly and distinctly, and (b) all together, not part by part. But, a deduction, when considered as about to be made, does not seem to take place all together. According to the exposition of Rule iii, *deductio* is a movement of the mind, inferring one thing from another. So *deductio* is rightly distinguished from and contrasted with *intuitus*. But, if we consider a deduction as already made, it is not a movement but the termination of a movement ('*nul lum motum . . . sed terminum motus*'[5]). Therefore, when the content deduced is simple and manifest, we suppose it to be seen by *intuitus*. When it is complex and involved, we take a different view, and give the process the name '*enumeratio*' or '*inductio*', because

[1] *Reg. xi*, A. & T., X, p. 407. Cp. *Reg. vii*, p. 389.
[2] Ibid., p. 390.
[3] Ibid., p. 389.
[4] Ibid., pp. 407-8.
[5] Ibid., p. 408.

the conclusion cannot be apprehended as a whole, and its certainty depends in part upon memory (i.e. it depends on judgements specified in many and various parts of the proof).

Yet, after all, if these passages only are considered, Descartes has shown no more than that, in complicated processes of reasoning, *enumeratio sive inductio* is a useful, indeed an indispensable, aid to proof. Induction is useful where the chain of reasoning is long, and in complex arguments where we have to lean more upon memory because the steps are too heterogenous to be perceived as a whole. A methodical grouping of these data and the numbering of the steps of the completed argument are necessary to prevent them from slipping from the memory or becoming disarranged. So far, then, *enumeratio* is not a mode of proof at all. Its function is to arrange and group premises already intuited and steps of an argument already deduced, in order to help retention in the memory. It is not a method by which to acquire fresh premises or to infer anything fresh from premises we already have.

But some other passages in the *Regulae* modify this position. In the exposition of Rule vii he says that this enumeration, or induction, is a scrutiny (*perquisitio*— a Baconian term) of everything relevant to the problem before us, careful and accurate enough for us to know that we have left out nothing of importance which ought to have been included; so that even if we fail to solve our problem we have advanced our knowledge at least to the extent that we perceive that the object for which we sought could not have been discovered by any method known to us. If we have surveyed all methods open to man, we may say that such knowledge is beyond the human mind.

This explains why Descartes often uses *enumeratio* as a preliminary survey of the ground before he attempts to solve a problem. For instance in the expositions of Rules viii and xii[1] we are given a survey of the implications of knowledge in regard to both possible objects of knowledge and possible instruments or powers of knowing. Both these passages are preliminary to an attempt to show the limits and range of the human intellect. Similarly in the exposition of Rule vii[2] the example is given of surveys preliminary to the proofs that the area of a circle is greater than that of any other figure of equal periphery, and that the rational soul is not corporeal.

Again in the Treatise on Dioptrics,[3] Descartes is about to explain the means of perfecting human vision: to determine what kinds, shapes and arrangements of lenses are most suitable for new optical instruments. He begins by saying that he wishes to make an enumeration of the improvements which art can supply, after enumerating the natural provisions: (i) bodies, the objects of vision; (ii) the interior organs receiving the action of these bodies, and (iii) the exterior organs, the eye and the media of vision, which dispose these objects so that their action can be properly received by the inner organs.

Descartes, then, considers these three heads one by one and makes the relevant distinctions; he discusses possible hindrances and aids, setting aside those which

[1] Ibid., pp. 395-6 and pp. 411-25.
[2] p. 390.
[3] A. & T., VI, pp. 147f.

are clearly impossible and estimating what obstacles and deficiencies cannot be removed by human knowledge.

These enumerations are clearly a preparatory mapping of the whole province of study, in some corners of which special investigation is to take place, and the solution of special problems to be found. The enumeration ensures that we see and consider whatever, in the province of the science as a whole, may be relevant to the special inquiry. In the wider domain there may be links essential to chains of reasoning required to solve the special problem (or problems). We must not disregard any link, or our subsequent conclusion may be invalidated.

But it is not easy to see how, on Descartes's theory, it is possible to make a preliminary survey at all. In the conduct of such surveys he does not say what our power of knowing is. A logical procedure is implied for which he does not seem to have allowed in his account of the intellect, as exhausted by *intuitus* and *deductio*. For preparatory surveys of this sort are of necessity general and abstract, and Descartes says they must be 'sufficient'—that is, to guard against the omission of anything which will be relevant to the problem subsequently investigated.[1] Further, they must be ordered—that is, conducted upon some principle—indeed any principle would do, provided it gave a comprehensive, convenient and time-saving arrangement. The enumerations are, therefore, always to some extent, and usually in the main, skeleton outlines; in fact, a sufficient enumeration need be little more than a disjunctive limitation of the gaps in our

[1] Cp. A. & T. X, pp. 389-90.

knowledge, while the connections between the data are known only in the barest outline.[1] The matters listed in the enumeration are included only as general groups; and within each subordinate group there is a plurality of singulars. But this internal detail is not specified and may be, as yet, unknown (either to anyone at all, or to us, the investigators at the moment), or may be known to be irrelevant to our special investigation and disregarded. So a general designation is all that need represent the group in our enumeration—it may be only an indeterminate negative; 'anything not-A'—and by this general designation we circumscribe an area left blank for our purposes, as a gap in knowledge, or a gap simply in our present knowledge, or merely an area seen to be irrelevant. It is a device by which we mark off an enemy fortress so that we can continue to advance, though we have not yet captured it.

In extreme cases a device of this kind would not be very helpful and would not enable us to pursue a profitable line of advance. Under some, or many, of the heads of the enumeration the subject matter may be so abstract or general that we cannot commit ourselves to any but superficial judgements. Descartes says[2] that only with the help of enumeration can we pass a certain judgement on any subject at all, and only with its help shall we know something about all the questions in our science. But, in many cases, this 'something' we should know may be so little that it is not worth mentioning.

[1] Cp. p. 390. ll. 13-18: Enumeration is merely auxiliary to the proof that the soul is not dependent upon the body.
[2] Ibid., p. 388.

Enumeratio is not, therefore, a method of proof at all. Descartes gives the name to two distinct devices: one for retaining in the memory the data from which inference has already been made; and the other a preliminary survey of the ground to select, compare and arrange the materials for an inference which is about to be made. The inference itself is always a movement of illation from one simple to another by the intellect —*deductio*. This passage (or transition) constitutes a linkage (or implication) which is self-evident, as are the inter-linked simples themselves. The linkage, in fact, is in principle identical with the nexus between *implicans* and *implicatum* within each single self-evident proposition.

Against this interpretation it may be said that Descartes frequently speaks of *inductio*, and, in one passage, of *imitatio*, suggesting that these are modes of proof other than *deductio* or *intuitus*. But he expressly identifies the power of knowing with *deductio* and *intuitus* alone.[1] Also he identifies *inductio* with specially intricate form of *deductio*, where the premises are complex or confused; and he gives no explanation of *imitatio* in connexion with *inductio*.

The one passage in which *imitatio* is mentioned[2] is very difficult, and since it has a bearing upon Descartes's method, we have good reason to examine it.

In actual inquiries we may sometimes come upon a link the implications of which, and therefore its immediate logical successor in the chain, are obscure, and advance is accordingly barred. There are two

[1] *Reg. xii*, p. 425, ll. 10-12.
[2] Cp. *Reg. viii*, pp. 393-5.

possible varieties of such situations: (i) The barrier may be absolute and insuperable owing to the limitation of the human mind.[1] (ii) The barrier may be insuperable only for those who confine themselves within the limits of a special science, but may be surmounted by those who pursue the universal aim of science and follow the principle of the Cartesian method. As stated under Rule I, the student's interest ought not to be confined to a single science, but he ought to study all. Descartes gives as an example the following problem:—

Suppose a student whose interest is confined to pure mathematics sets out to discover the line of refraction in optics. Such a student will follow the method of analysis and synthesis, set out in Rules v and vi, and will see that the determination of this line depends upon the relation between the angles of incidence and the angles of refraction.[2] He will recognize that the discovery of this requires a knowledge of physics and is impossible for the pure mathematician, so he will break off his inquiry.

But now suppose a student whose aim is universal: he will desire to pass a true judgement here also, and, as a genuine student of all the sciences, he will be able to complete the analysis, proceeding until he reaches the simplest link in the implicatory sequence involved in the problem. He will find that the ratio varies in accordance with the variation in the angles resulting from changes in the physical media, and that these again are dependent upon the mode of propaga-

[1] Vide *Reg. viii*, p. 396. No example is given though he says that many such cases may occur.
[2] Cp. *La Dioptrique* A. & T. VI, pp. 100-1, 211-214.

tion of the rays of light. He will find that knowledge of this propagation requires a knowledge of the nature of illumination; and that again presupposes the knowledge of what a natural force, or energy, is. In the last presupposition the student has reached the simplest link in the implicatory sequence (for this problem), and, having gained a clear insight, he will now (in accordance with Rule v) begin his synthesis link by link.

If now he finds himself unable to perceive the nature of illumination, he will enumerate all the other forms of natural force (in accordance with Rule vii), so that he may understand, at least by the analogy 'imitatio') of what he knows of the other natural forces. Descartes promises a later explanation of *imitatio*, but this promise remains unfulfilled, probably because the *Regulae* was never completed. He seems to have in mind a process of hypothetical construction, in this instance, of the nature of illumination by analogy from the nature of some other natural force which is known to the inquirer and which it may be supposed to resemble.[1]

[1] Cf. *Reg. xiv*, A. & T. X, pp. 438-9.

CHAPTER II

THE CARTESIAN METHOD

★

R U L E I V : We have next to consider why a method is necessary for investigating the truth of things, what it can hope to do and on what rules it should proceed. The method is explained and justified in the first half of the exposition of Rule iv.[1] Owing to the origin of Descartes's conception of method he tends to confuse it with science and is led to speak of his new science of order and measure.[2] The second half of the exposition[3] is devoted to an account of this, and here Descartes explains how he himself came to discover it, and the passage is largely autobiographical. In the Hanover MS. it comes at the end of the *Regulae*, but even there a note to Rule iv refers to it.[4]

Descartes tells us in the exposition of Rule vii that Rules v, vi and vii should be taken together; that all three contribute equally to the perfection of the method, and that 'the rest of the treatise' (presumably Rules viii - xi, for from Rule xii onward a different

---

[1] A. & T., X, pp. 371-4.
[2] Cp. below pp. 81ff.
[3] A.&T., X, pp. 374-379.
[4] Ibid., p. 374 n.a.

subject matter is treated) does little more than work out in detail what they cover in general. In the discussion of *enumeratio* we have already dealt with Rule vii, so we may now consider the exposition of Rule iv[1] and Rules v and vi.[2]

Descartes says that nearly all chemists, most geometers and the majority of philosophers pursue their studies haphazard without any method at all. Occasionally these aimless studies lead accidentally to truth, but these coincidental cases are more than outweighed by the serious injury done by such procedure to the mind, because vague and confused studies weaken the natural light. That is why people with little or no learning are often far superior in forming clear and sound judgements on the ordinary matters of life.

By a method he means certain and easy rules such that anyone who precisely obeys them will never take for truth anything that is false, and will advance step by step, in the correct order without waste of mental energy, to the knowledge of everything that he is capable of knowing. But he suggests that it is not the method which enables us to know, for it is the nature of the intellect to perceive what is clear and distinct and also to move infallibly from one self-evident link to the next, along the line of logical implication. Not only are *intuitus* and *deductio* the sole means of knowing—this they must be in order to be *vis cognoscens* at all—but we could not *learn* to use them, because we should have to use them in order to learn, and unless we both possess and use them from the first we could get nowhere. But, says Descar-

[1] pp. 371-2.
[2] pp. 379-87.

tes, if we use the method, we can increase, guide and exercise the powers of *intuitus* and *deductio*. We can so arrange the materials, on which our power of intellectual vision is to be turned, and the links which are to form the stages of illation, that our natural powers will work under the most favourable conditions and will develop in scope and in intensity.

The general principles of the method are set out in Rules v, vi and vii and the details in Rules ix, x and xi : Those applying to *intuitus* come under Rule ix, those concerning *deductio*, in more complex cases, under Rule x, and those applying to cases where both together and concomitantly are to be used, under Rule xi.

The entire method consists in the ordering and arrangement of material on which attention is to be concentrated. Exact observance of it will be secured if we reduce involved and complex propositions to simple ones and begin by exercising our intellect (*intuitus*)[1] on the simple, and then work our way up step by step to all the others. In the exposition of this Rule, Descartes emphasises its supreme importance.[2] Here as elsewhere, he warns us against the neglect of the simple and easy. Many scientists, he says, have a tendency to attack the most intricate problems before they have resolved the more elementary difficulties; and philosophers also neglect the obvious facts of experience.

But though this advice is undeniably sound, the difficulty is to carry it out. How can we reduce the

[1] '*Ex omnium simplicissimarum intuitu*' means 'insight into the simplest propositions of all', not 'all the simplest propositions'.
[2] Cp. *Reg. ii*, p. 364, *Reg. iii*, p. 368 and *Reg. x*, p. 401-3.

complex to the simple? How are we to recognize the degrees of simplicity in the results of our analysis? How may we arrange them in the right order and know what is the simplest proposition of all when we reach it? Rule vi professes to give us the answer.[1]

At this point the doctrine of the *Regulae* has taken a new turn, and the details of this new development are difficult and obscure. Its general tendency is hard, if at all possible, to reconcile with the theory which has hitherto been attributed to Descartes and into which at last he unintentionally relapses. So far, Descartes has said that in every investigation our aim must be to transform all complex propositions[2] into an intelligible combination of simple elements, so clear to the intellect that they can be directly known. We must reconstitute the complex in terms of the simple and self-evident. Every proposition must be resolved by analysis into simple or elementary constituents, and then resynthesized in an order which makes their relations and implications transparent to the intellect. This doctrine is a familiar one in philosophy, but the criticism of it is also familiar. The kind of analysis demanded is usually, or perhaps always, impossible, not simply because of the weakness of our intelligence, but in the nature of the case. For it is not true that all, or most, complex facts could be known if treated in this way. Few complex facts, if any, are sums or combinations of isolable and externally re-

---

[1] *Vide* pp. 381, l. 8 and 382, ll. 17-19.

    N.B. Baillet omits Rule vi in his popular summary of the *Regulae*. In Adam & Tannery his words on Rule v are mistakenly referred to Rule vi.

[2] Austin has 'every complex problem'. (Ed.).

lated constituents and to conceive them as such would not be knowledge but error. But how are we to reconcile with such a theory the doctrine of method now to be maintained, a doctrine underlying Rule v and worked out in Rule vi?

According to this doctrine the method still, no doubt, consists as before entirely in analysis and synthesis, but we now learn that these operations are gradual and their results graduated. It is not simples that are combined to form a complex. The complex is the last in a series of terms which gradually grow in complexity: it is the end of a long development at the beginning of which is the simple, or alternatively, the simple is the limit of a process of progressive reduction or gradual simplification of the complex, into increasingly simple propositions and terms, continued until the ('absolute') simplest proposition of all is reached. Synthesis starts from this and advances through the stages of the reductive (analytic) process in the reverse order. So it issues in more and more complicated propositions and terms until it ends in the original complex—but now reconstituted as a clearly intelligible and demonstrated conclusion deduced from the early less complex propositions and terms.

Thus, according to these new rules, the process of analysis is continuous and proceeds to the absolutely simple, while the synthesis is a progressive reconstruction beginning from the simple and going through the increasing degrees of complexity until it ends in the original complex from which the analysis started.

So far as we can judge, this new conception—of degrees of simplicity or complexity—is not consistent with the former conception which Descartes has been maintaining and which he, nevertheless, continues to maintain to the end. There is only one field where the two views seem, and perhaps are, compatible—that of number, from which alone Descartes takes his examples.[1]

RULE VI. The Latin here is faulty but the meaning is clear. If we are to distinguish the most simple things from the most complex and to advance in the right order, we must proceed as follows: taking any sequence of truths deduced one from another, we must observe which is the simplest and how the rest are related to it—whether more, or less, or equally removed from it.

The exposition is obscure. As the Rule states, things can be arranged in certain series. They are not to be considered as separate and independent in character, nor is the arrangement of them in series to be regarded as a grouping under Aristotelian categories or different kinds of being. What is meant is the connection of things in their logical relations, so far as the knowledge of one can be derived from that of another (or others), things related *qua implicantia* and *implicata*. The series are implicatory sequences.

In every such series the terms may be distinguished according as they are either absolute or relative, independent or derivative. If relative or dependent they may be distinguished in respect to the kind and degree of their dependence. In each sequence there is a first term, on which all the rest depend but which is independent of them; a second term dependent on the first but not on the rest, though all others depend upon

[1] *Vide* pp. 384-7 and 409-410.

it. The implication is always unilateral and not reciprocal. A proposition (for Descartes) may be necessary,
even though its converse is contingent.[1]

Further, 'absolute' and 'relative' turn out to be
themselves relative terms in this connection. A term
may be absolute from one point of view and relative
from another. It may be more or less absolute or
relative. 'Absolute' and 'relative' are to be understood
with reference to the subject under investigation.

A term is absolute in the highest sense, if it contains
the 'nature'[2] under investigation in its purest and most
simple form. This is the limit of the analysis and so the
first term in the re-synthesis. So in the series of steps
leading to the discovery of the line of refraction, the
last term of regressive analysis—or first of the progressive re-synthesis—is 'natural energy'. Now this is
absolute in relation to the second term, *illuminatio*,
because it stands to it as universal to particular.
'Natural energy' or 'force in general' is an abstract
universal in which heat, light, etc., etc., all share in
various ways. But in other examples, the contrast
between two terms as absolute and relative may depend on one or other of a variety of antitheses[3]:
simple as opposed to complex, similar as opposed to

---

[1] Cp. *Reg. xi*, p. 422. The relations of successive terms in such an
implicatory sequence are indicated by Descartes and Spinoza
by certain technical terms. The absolute and independent is
related to the relative and derivative as 'Substance' to 'Mode',
and the relatively more independent to the relatively more dependent as 'primary mode' to 'subordinate mode'.

[2] Descartes's use of the term '*natura*', here and elsewhere, is vague
(vide pp. 382, ll. 3-4; 383, l. 3; 440, ll. 10-20). It is perhaps
reminiscent of Bacon.

[3] Cp. pp. 381-2.

68

dissimilar, straight as opposed to oblique. But (and this is the real crux) whatever the antithesis, we must remember that the point of the contrast is always the order of logical implication. It is the absolutely or relatively *known*, not the absolutely or relatively *existent*, with which we are concerned. Thus in the case of cause and effect, in existence they are correlative, but in knowledge the effect presupposes the cause, which is thus prior in the implicatory sequence. Similarly unequal, dissimilar, oblique, presuppose the knowledge of equal, similar, straight (though not their existence or reality) and so come **after** them in the implicatory series; i.e. they are τῷ λόγῳ ὕστερα καὶ πρότερα (Descartes clearly has Aristotle's distinction in mind).

In every investigation of a complex problem, therefore, we must gradually reduce it to the most absolute term, pressing on with the regressive analysis until we reach the term which is first in this sense. On this we must concentrate our mental vision until we have a perfect and thorough mental insight. We can then begin a reconstructive synthesis, correctly arranging the terms of the implicatory sequence, which issues in the solution of the problem.

All the terms, except the first, are called by Descartes 'relative' ('*respectiva*'), because every one of them implies the first, and the conception of them presupposes as a condition the 'real' or 'nature', which is embodied in the first or absolute term. They are derived from it by a continuous deductive chain and embody it in part. But they include also other elements or features, and if we are to conceive them adequately, we must take these added determinants into account

69

as well as the absolute nature. Descartes calls these other elements '*respectus*' and they are dependent upon relations to other things in other implicatory sequences. Thus even the least relative of the relative terms contains, in the adequate conception of it, a feature that restricts the simple nature of the absolute term. This feature is a respect, or regard, connecting it with (and making it relevant to) another sequence.

As the synthetic series proceeds, the successive terms grow in complexity and each contains more and more of these *respectus*, or references beyond itself; they grow in complexity or concreteness. But this means that there is a continuous addition of fresh determinants—more and more features are added as the series advances—and each of these is a relative term connecting it with an absolute belonging to another sequence. So every relative or complex term in a series is the meeting-point of two or more implicatory sequences, each of which, if followed up, would lead to its own absolute term,[1] and the mind must combine a number of features in conceiving each of the relative terms.

So the analysis and synthesis of Descartes's method yield a number of implicatory sequences, each involving a number of terms which grow in complexity as the sequence advances. In each the first term is a simple nature—a certain feature of reality in its purity—and each successive term is derivative from this first one. The subsequent terms each contain this along with other added features which relate the first to other, different implicatory sequences. In other

[1] *Vide*, p. 382, ll. 3-16.

words, there are (i) the simplest, primary and most absolute terms, and (ii) a number of increasingly less simple, more complex, derivative terms.

The first point to be criticized is that the contrast between absolute and relative terms in every sequence is, in fact, based on one principle only (though Descartes says that there are more). It is always by subtraction that the terms become more simple in analysis and can be arranged in a progressively more simple series, and it is only by addition that they become progressively more complex in synthesis. If X is a simpler term and Y more complex, Y will always contain X plus something else in addition. If X's character is precisely α, then the character of Y is $\alpha + \beta$; and if there is a third term Z, more relative and complex than Y, this can only mean, according to Descartes, that the character of Z is $(\alpha + \beta) + \gamma$.

Descartes enumerates, it is true, several apparently different antitheses and asserts that any one may serve as the basis of the distinction between absolute and relative terms in a given sequence. It may be that Y is related to X as particular to universal, or as effect to cause, or as composite to simple, or as oblique to straight. But, in fact, his account of the order of terms always assumes that they are related to one another according to the above scheme: i.e., α; $\alpha + \beta$; $(\alpha + \beta) + \gamma$., etc., as if the only antithesis that could serve as a basis for relativity were between the abstract universal and that same abstract universal plus added determinants.

This result seems to follow inevitably from Descartes's statements and it suggests three comments:

(i) In the synthetic implicatory sequence the successive terms do not become less simple, or more complex as the sequence proceeds, in any genuine sense. They may appear so, but when examined they will always reduce to absolute simples related by an absolutely simple connexion. It is always a case of less or more constituents and the more numerous constituents do not make the relative term really more complex as to the nature of the constituents or the manner of aggregation. The larger aggregate is not more developed in the mode of relation of its elements. Successive terms do not grow in concreteness, they are not genuinely one, or whole at all. Further, they do not even exhibit increasing complexity of structure. For example, 7 is not more complex than 6, if 6 is nothing more than the five-fold addition of 1 to 1 and 7 the six-fold operation.

So we come back to the original form of Descartes's method. It remains, as always, the resolution of a complex into absolute simples simply related—a sum or aggregate. If any term in the process of synthesis or analysis seems to be more simple than another, that only means that the work of the scientist or philosopher has not yet been completed. We are grasping confusedly what, if perceived clearly, would be seen as an aggregate of simples, and confusing it with a genuinely concrete fact—that is, a term genuinely single (in the sense that it can't be split up without being altered) yet not atomic.

(ii) At every step there is a break in logical continuity. This is obvious in the synthetic reconstruction of the sequence, for each successive term adds a feature, to its predecessor, new in the sense that it is logically discontinuous and irrelevant to what went before.

And this new '*respectus*' refers the mind away along a different implicatory sequence to a different absolute term which the new determinant involves.

(iii) To what field or fields of fact (or reality) can such a method be applied with any prospect of yielding knowledge? What kind of facts could it explain and not explain away? Obviously, it can apply only to a field where every fact is either atomic and simple or an aggregate of simples. Such a method, then, is powerless to deal with such matters as the phenomena of life, and *a fortiori* with the domain of philosophy— the field of conscious, or self-conscious, spirit or thought.

At first sight the objects of arithmetic and algebra, number and numerical proportion only, seem to satisfy the required conditions. They alone are such as to be explained, and not distorted or explained away, by the sort of reasoning guided by the rules of the Cartesian method. All applied mathematics, geometry and the whole of the rest of nature, animate and inanimate, because they involve continuity and movement, must elude the grasp of the method, and what Descartes says is sound reasoning. As for the spiritual facts of ethics, aesthetics or logic and all that are studied by philosophy, it seems ludicrous to suppose that any light could be thrown on them by a reasoning based on the assumption that they are aggregates of simples. If so, the method is worthless in philosophy and of little or no use in any science except arithmetic and algebra.

But we must consider what can be said against this criticism and we shall find that a strong case can be made both on general grounds and by reference to

Descartes's own view of the relation between mathematics and philosophy

1. *General objections to the criticism.* Many philosophers besides Descartes and all, or most, men of science would agree that analysis can be nothing else than the resolution of the complex into simples. Doubtless there are facts in our experience which stand out against such treatment and resist analysis; which if so treated seem to have been explained away. But that means (they say) only that some facts are inexplicable and must always remain unintelligible just because they cannot be analysed. Or they might say that it may mean, or does mean in most cases, that some facts are so complex that they are beyond our present powers of analysis—outside the reach of the longest chains of implicatory sequence we can construct. Nevertheless, they would claim, no more is needed than patience and persistence for analysis along the same lines to resolve even such complex cases. For, they would ask, what kind of analysis other than this could there be? What new method of procedure can be conceived? If there is such a method, it must be one which explains the concrete fact without analysis or resolution into simples, and it should be produced. In effect, the critic is challenged to show that any mode of reasoning, other than analysis by subtraction and synthesis by addition, is possible.

2. *Descartes's special rejoinder.* Descartes not only shares the position on which these general objections are founded, but he also maintains a theory of mathematics and of its relation to philosophy which cuts the

74

ground from under the feet of the critic and seriously undermines his position. According to this theory, the method controlling mathematical reasoning, in its purest, most abstract and general form—the proper method of the science as Descartes conceives it—is *eo ipso* the method which our reason must use for knowledge in every field of the knowable. In the case of one field only does Descartes make an exception—that of self-conscious mind. Notions of extension, motion, figure, number, etc., comprising the whole of nature up to and including man's animal nature fall within the scope of mathematical reasoning. The sciences and the branches of philosophy which are concerned with these fields of being are nothing but off-shoots and developments of the supreme science; they are the expansion of the same spirit which produces as its first fruits the universal principles of order and measure, which Descartes identifies with true mathematics, and which he calls '*mathesis universalis*', as opposed to '*mathematica vulgaris*.

The student of philosophy who is not a mathematician hesitates to discuss this subject, but it is one of fundamental importance for the understanding of Descartes's philosophy, especially the *Regulae*; and anybody who wishes to make a serious effort and to form a just estimate of his doctrine must deal with it.

What were the aim, scope and value of this universal science? Without the answer to this question even the exposition in the *Discourse on Method*[1] is not clear, and *a fortiori* that in the *Regulae* is not. Also, the primary significance of Descartes's theory is philosophical, and the strict mathematician, in his admira-

[1] Cp. A. & T., VI, pp. 17-20.

tion of the technical details, may fail to see the wood for the trees.[1]

Descartes's conception of method was derived originally from reflection upon the procedure of arithmeticians and geometricians. He was deeply impressed by the self-evident certainty of their reasoning and the ease with which it could solve abstruse, complex and intricate problems. He thought he had discovered the principles to which it owed its success, and his formulation of what he took these principles to be constituted his method in its earliest form. But he soon realized that his own methods, which he had used in doing this were much better than the actual reasonings of the geometers and arithmeticians, by reflection upon which he had formulated the principles. In these reasonings he became aware of defects; they were not logically continuous movements of thought along single lines of implicatory sequences, and the existing mathematical systems were not logically consistent and coherent as he conceived science should be.[2]

The substance of his criticism is that the proofs are of the 'mousetrap' variety—the reader is tricked into agreement by some careless admission or even some extraneous absurdity imported into the argument,and is not really convinced. The argument does not in clude, as its middle term, the real bond of connection between premises and conclusion—the real nexus inherent in the subject-matter—its appeal is to the eye or the imagination rather than to the intellect—and if

[1] Cp. Liard, *Descartes* (Paris, 1882), pp. 8-10, 35-63.
[2] *Vide* supra pp. 25-28, and Cp. Descartes's dissatisfaction with *Mathematica Vulgaris*, both as to subject-matter and method, expressed in *Reg.* iv., *Expl.* pp. 374-8.

the student is convinced, it is not by the so-called proof, but by his own independent insight. Hence education based on arithmetic and geometry alone, by concentrating attention on such spurious and superficial demonstrations,[1] actually tends to weaken the intellect by allowing its natural powers of *intuitus* and *deductio* to atrophy.[2] Descartes is also severe in his condemnation of the futility of the problems actually set in the contemporary mathematics.[3] Nothing, he says, can be more futile than to devote oneself to the study of bare numbers and imaginary[4] figures, as though the whole aim of life were the knowledge of such things.[5] His point is that such studies are only valuable as a preliminary to physics—or the philosophy of nature—the more concrete study of the natural world, though mathematicians make extravagant claims for their collections of increasingly intricate problems and ingenious solutions, which are of no more than technical interest, and make no contribution to furthering the knowledge of nature.

But the defects of the contemporary mathematics, Descartes is convinced, were, so to say, accidental. The fault lay not with mathematics but with the mathematicians—not in the essential nature of the science, but in the mistakes of individual scientists. He believes that there is a *vera mathesis* which, being

[1] *Vide Reg. iv*, p. 375.
[2] Cp. Schopenhauer's 'Four-fold proof of sufficient reason'. But his position is different in so far as he holds that, in geometry, the only adequate and genuine proof is, and must be, the appeal to spatial intuition.
[3] *Reg. iv*, pp. 371 and 375.
[4] Meaning 'imaginable' or 'pictured in the imagination'.—Ed.
[5] *Vide* p. 375.

the simplest, is the foundation of all knowledge—a mathematics which is the necessary propaedeutic for the mastery of science and philosophy by the mind. That there must be such a science existing, so to speak, *in posse*, waiting to be discovered, follows, Descartes thinks, from the very nature of his method, and its existence, in some manner, must have been known, at least in outline, to the great mathematicians of antiquity.

For this method, two conditions must be fulfilled: we must accept as true only what is self-evident, and we must follow the correct logical expansion of these data. Only thus will the intellect be following the procedure dictated by its own true nature. This is consistent with another conviction of Descartes's, that there are certain seeds of truth implanted by nature in our minds;[1] and he speaks of 'inborn principles of method' bearing 'spontaneous fruits.[2] They are seeds which tend to ripen spontaneously in a natural harvest of knowledge, that tends to develop along certain lines, which, if made definite and formulated as rules of guidance, are the Cartesian method. We must note, in passing, the following important points:

(i) In the exposition of Rule iv, the development of knowledge is expressed in terms of the mind's attentive observation of ideas in itself and their natural

[1] Cp. *Reg. iv*, pp. 373 and 376, and *Discours* (A. & T. VI), p. 64. The doctrine may be traced back to Aquinas, *De Veritate*: '*Praeexistant in nobis quaedam scientiarum semina*' (*Quaestiones Disputatae, De Veritate, Quaestio xii, art I.*).

[2] Loc. cit. (p. 373): '. . . *spontaneae fruges ex ingenitis hujus methodi principiis natae* . . .'

expansion and development. The 'seeds' are implanted and are data given to the immediate seeing of the mind. As they are given they are also received, and reception is a determinate mode of the mind's innate functioning—to see *this*, is to see it *thus* (somehow). Thus Descartes has already formed and is already working with the same conception of 'idea' as appears in his later teaching.[1]

(ii) The emphasis laid here on growth and the metaphor of seeds ripening to maturity take the place of the metaphor of links in a chain. We must not, however, rashly assume that Descartes would have regarded increment or growth as anything other than addition. Aristotle distinguished αὔξησις from πρόσθεσις but we have no reason to suppose that Descartes would have done the same.

He asserts in the exposition of Rule iv,[2] that so far as the easiest of all sciences (Arithmetic and Geometry) are concerned there is positive evidence that germinal truths in the mind have spontaneously ripened and produced a harvest of knowledge. The old Greek geometers employed analysis in all problems, though they jealously kept the method secret; and the modern, flourishing algebra also attempts to apply to numbers the same sort of analysis as the Ancients applied to figures. Later,[3] he says more positively that traces of the *vera mathesis* are apparent in the works of Pappus

[1] Cp. esp. the end of answer to the Second set of Objections, A. & T. VII, p. 160.
[2] A. & T., X, p. 373.
[3] Ibid., p. 376.

and Diophantus.[1] But the analysis of the old Greek geometers and the algebra of Descartes's time are very imperfect anticipations of his own *vera mathesis*, as he himself observes in the *Discourse on Method*.[2] He complains that the ancients are so tied down to special figures that their work too narrowly restricts the exercise of the mind; and that the contemporary algebra seems, with its obscure symbols, rather to embarrass the mind than to clarify. This passage in the *Discours* is obviously based on Rule iv,[3] stating the same opinion more clearly, in a shorter, more elegant and more popular form.[4] In the passage of the *Regulae*,[5] he says that algebra lacks the supreme clearness and facility which should characterise *vera mathesis* as a genuine embodiment of the method.

Vera Mathesis. What, however, is this *vera mathesis*? As Descartes describes it and as he elaborates and uses it for his philosophy of nature, it is an amalgamation of two heterogeneous elements, which are contributed by two different and discrepant faculties.

[1] Cp. Heath, *History of Greek Mathematics* II, pp. 400-401, for Pappus' definition of analysis. Hamelin says (*Le Systeme de Descartes*, p. 7) that Vieta was responsible, more than any other, for casting geometrical problems in the form of equations; but Descartes did not read him until 1629 (after the *Regulae* had been written). Vieta owed most to Diophantus.

[2] Cp. A. & T., VI, pp. 17-18 and p. 549.

[3] A. & T., X, pp. 375-7.

[4] The Latin version of the *Discours* is better than the French. Descartes himself corrected and revised it and requested that it be regarded as the original.

[5] *Reg. iv*, p. 377.

(i) As a science proper it is purely intellectual (as, for Descartes, all science must be)—intellect expressing and fulfilling itself in act—with a purely abstract, intelligible domain. But (ii) the imagination co-operates with the intellect and, though Descartes regards it as only instrumental to the work of the intellect, yet to the imagination and its contributions are due the whole value of the *vera mathesis* for the science of nature, and its entire originality.

Descartes's conception of *vera mathesis*, considered as a science, and of its domain as the subject-matter of a science, is stated very clearly in the autobiographical passage in the exposition to Rule iv.[1] He says that when his thoughts turned from the special sciences of arithmetic and geometry to the idea of universal mathematics, he first asked himself what is meant by the term 'mathematics', and why many sciences, such as optics, mechanics, astronomy, etc. are commonly reckoned as parts of mathematics. What is common to all these despite their different subject-matters? How can the beginner at once see what belongs to mathematics—what makes an investigation mathematical? After careful consideration, he says, he came to the conclusion that inquiries in which order and measure are examined, and these alone, are referred to mathematical science—it matters not whether in numbers, figures, sounds or stars. There must, then, be a science relating to order and measure, as such, in general, and abstracted from their relation to this or that special subject-matter; and this alone is entitled to be called *mathesis universalis* or *vera mathesis*. Geometry, arithmetic, etc. are only called

[1] pp. 377-8. Cp. *Reg. vi*, p. 385, ll. 1-4.

mathematics in so far as they each deal with a part of the domain of universal mathematics.

The same doctrine is expressed more shortly in the *Discours*.[1] All the mathematical sciences, he says there, are concerned with a common object of investigation: the relations or proportions obtaining within their special subjects. The domain, then, of pure mathematics is that of proportion as such or in general. *Vera mathesis* or *mathesis universalis* is, therefore, the Cartesian method directly applied to a systematic investigation of all problems connected with proportion, order and measure, conceived as such and in general, in abstraction from the particular things in the subject-matter which bear these proportions.

The terms used in both the *Regulae* and the *Discours* 'order', 'measure' and 'dimension', are technical terms in the new *vera mathesis*. Descartes gives a somewhat sketchy account of them in the exposition of Rule xiv.[2] 'Dimension' is any aspect of a perceptible, picturable or imaginable object in respect of which it is measurable; including, for example, weight and velocity (the dimensions of motion). Order applies to a manifold (*Menge*)[3] and measure only to a continuous magnitude. The latter can always be reduced to a manifold, *saltem ex parte*, by the help of an assumed unit, and the many so obtained can then be ordered

[1] A. & T., VI, pp. 19-20, 550-1.
[2] pp. 447-52.
[3] Austin's version has 'manner', which is surely due to a mishearing of the German word '*Menge*'; though why Joachim should have drawn attention to the German equivalent is not clear. Presumably, he had Kant's usage in mind: cp. *Kritik der Reinen Vernunft*, A.103, 163 and B.204. (Ed.).

in such a way as to facilitate measurement of the magnitude. In the more popular summary in the *Discours*, Descartes substitutes the less technical term 'proportion'.

So far, there is nothing original in Descartes's *vera mathesis* and nothing very promising for the solution of problems in the physical sciences or for their future development. The idea of mathematics so specialized is familiar to Aristotle,[1] who makes it clear that the Greek mathematicians of his day had developed a theory of proportion in general. He refers to the theory that proportions alternate and says that this theory used to be demonstrated in detachments for the different species of proportionate things (numbers, lengths, durations, etc.) But (says Aristotle) alternation is true of all proportionals, in virtue of their common character and is not dependent on the features in which they are specifically distinct from one another. Hence, nowadays, (he continues) the mathematicians postulate something present in all proportionate things and say that alternation is characteristic of this something, being universally predicable of it.

Reverting, then, to Descartes's attack on the vulgar mathematics, we can now see one feature of his criticism more clearly. The intelligible domain of mathematics—the only proper subject of the *vera mathesis*, as a science—is proportions *qua* proportions, or proportion in general, which does not alter with the subjects which it informs, and must be abstracted from its particular embodiments. Among these subjects are numbers and figures; but the vulgar mathematicians, says Descartes, miss the substance and pur-

[1] *Metaphysics* 1026a26-27, and *An. Post.* 74a17-25.

sue the shadow.[1] On the other hand, the Greeks and the contemporary algebraists did attempt to grapple with the proper subject of the science and with *what is embodied* in figures and numbers, but they failed to realise that proportions, as such, have nothing to do with the figures and numbers in which they happen to be enwrapped. There is no need to be tied down to figures (like the Greeks) or to numbers (like the algebraists). So in place of a general theory, these thinkers produced theories appropriate to each separate field, and they were able really to grapple with proportions only in those two domains of number and figure. The proper business of *vera mathesis*, however, is to treat proportion in abstraction from numbers and figures as well from all other embodiments.[2]

The rôle of the imagination in *vera mathesis* is summarised in the *Discours*,[3] where, though Descartes skates over the difficulties, he gives a clearer general view than in his more elaborate and contorted account in the *Regulae*. He says that he is determined to study proportions in general without referring them to any objects in particular; but he intends to use some objects to aid the intellect and facilitate understanding. He would, he decided, sometimes have to study each kind of embodiment of proportion apart from the others, and sometimes many at once, keeping them in mind by means of memory. When he comes to consider proportions separately, in abstracto, he thinks it best to study them '*tantum in lineis rectis*', for,

[1] Cp. *Reg. iv*, pp. 373 *ad fin.*, esp. pp. 374-7.
[2] Cp. *Reg. xiv*, p. 452, ll. 14-26, and *Reg. xvi*, p. 455 *ad fin.*, (esp. p. 456).
[3] A. & T., VI, p. 20 and p. 551.

he says, he can find nothing simpler than straight lines, or better adapted to represent proportions distinctly to the senses or the imagination. But to study many kinds of proportion together he had decided to use various symbols—letters and numerals—algebraical formulae, the notation of which he has explained elsewhere.[1] This would embody all that is best in the Greek geometers, as well as the work of the algebraists, while it supplied the deficiencies and corrected the errors of both.

But for a proper appreciation of the use of imagination in *vera mathesis* we must refer to the more complicated account in the *Regulae*.[2] Descartes is here explaining the plan of the whole of the *Regulae*. He says that all possible objects of knowledge may be divided into simple proportions, on the one hand, and problems (*quaestiones*) on the other. The former must present themselves spontaneously to the mind. They are identical with data. There are no rules for the discovery of simple proportions, nor are they to be found by deliberate search. All we can do is to give the intellect certain precepts for training the powers of knowing in general, rules which will make it see more clearly and scrutinize more carefully the objects presented to it. These are covered by Rules i-xii, while '*quaestiones*' are to form the subject matter of the remaining rules. Rules xiii and xxiv will deal with '*quaestiones quae perfecte intelliguntur*' (i.e. those fully understood, both as to their terms and their solutions, even though the actual solutions are not yet known) and Rules xxv onward are to deal with

[1] Cp. *Reg. xvi*, pp. 454-9.
[2] *Reg. xii*, pp. 428-9.

'quaestiones quae imperfecte intelliguntur' (i.e. those problems not perfectly understood, but obscure in relation to some of the terms in which they are formulated and some of the conditions relevant to solution).

Descartes gradually unfolds his doctrine, starting from general considerations applying to both kinds of problem.[1] In every problem there must be something unknown, which must be somehow designated—that is, referred to something known. This is true of all problems, perfect or imperfect. Suppose that we set out to inquire what is the nature of a magnet (imperfect). The meaning of the terms 'nature' and 'magnet' must be known, and by these *cognita* the search is restricted and determined to a solution of a certain kind.

All imperfect problems can be reduced to perfect, but the rules for doing this, which Descartes says will be given in the proper place,[2] were never completed. (We may conjecture how this may be done from what he says in the exposition of Rule xiii). We may take completed experiments and argue from them as fixed facts, or data, the imperfect question thus becoming perfect. For instance, we may reformulate our previous question and ask what must be inferred about the nature of a magnet from Gilbert's experiments. We know the precise nature of Gilbert's experiments, and the *quaesitum* is now that solution which is individually determined by reference to these data and to them alone. What (we must ask) is the necessary inference (neither more nor less) from these

[1] *Vide Reg. xiii*, pp. 430-38.
[2] Ibid, p. 431 (i.e. *Reg. xxv-xxxvi*).

cognita. But Descartes further maintains that not only can an imperfect problem be reduced to a perfect one, but every perfect problem can or ought to be further reduced until it becomes one belonging to the domain of *vera mathesis*—i.e. one concerning proportions, order and measure alone. The reduction of a problem is not complete, or a problem is not strictly perfect, until it has become purely and abstractly mathematical. So we must go on refining our *cognita* until we are no longer studying this or that matter in which proportions are embodied, but are concerned only with comparing sheer magnitudes.[1] Accordingly, Descartes says, pure or perfect problems occur only in arithmetic and geometry.

The necessity of this reduction of problems, to questions of pure, universal mathematics, follows from the inherent nature of the intellect,[2] its limitations as well as its positive capacities. The exposition of Rule xiv, throws further light upon the distinction between absolute and relative terms in the implicatory sequence. Here he points out that obviously we cannot by sheer reasoning discover a new kind of being or nature. If from the known we deduce an unknown, all that our new knowledge involves is the perception that the unknown (*res quaesita*) participates, in this or that way, in the nature of the known data. To reason to a new kind of entity would be as impossible as to argue a man blind from birth into perceiving true ideas of colours; though Descartes admits that it might be possible for a man who had seen the primary

[1] *Vide Reg. xiii*, p. 431, ll 15-27 and cp. *Reg. xiv*, p. 441, ll. 21-29, and *Reg. xvii*, p. 459, ll. 10-15.
[2] Cp. *Reg. xiv*, *Expl.* pp. 438-40.

colours to construct for himself intermediate colours by 'a kind of deduction based on similarity' (*imitatio*?) If a magnet had a nature quite unlike any we had ever perceived we could reach it only by means of some new sense, or of a mind like God's. The utmost that the human mind could achieve would be to perceive distinctly that combination of known natures which would produce observed effects.

According to the doctrine here implied, the intellect presupposes, as the condition of its deductive movement, an already existing knowledge of certain kinds of objects (or natures). Descartes has said that the mind must deduce from an immediately apprehended, purely intelligible datum; but what he has in mind here, is not this, nor such a purely intelligible insight as he mentions in the *Discourse on Method*. The sort of knowledge he is thinking of, here, is a kind of sensuous or imaginative apprehension. In order to deduce, the intellect must start from and move within a nature that is known in the same sort of way as an object which is presented to sense. That this is his meaning becomes clear when one observes how the argument proceeds. In a case like that of the magnet, such previously known natures are, for example, extension, figure, motion, etc., each of which is such that it is recognized in every object and is seen as the same idea in all its embodiments—we picture (*imaginamus*)[1] the shape of a crown always by means of the same idea, whether it be made of silver or gold. This idea is transferred from one body to another by virtue of simple comparison, and the comparison must be 'simple and open', if the inferred conclusion is to

[1] *Vide* ibid., p. 439.

be true. But the comparison of two things *is* simple and manifest only when they contain a nature equally. Hence, all inferential knowledge (i.e. all proper knowledge other than *intuitus*) is obtained by the comparison of two or more things; and if our knowledge is to be precise, we must so formulate and purify our problem that we perceive the *quaesitum* as like, equal to, or identical with, the datum in respect of some nature contained in both.

Before the problem is properly formulated the terms are not directly comparable. *Quaesitum* and *cognitum* do not exhibit a common character which is seen to be equal by simple inspection and comparison. As the problem is first stated, the common nature is contained in the terms unequally or enwrapped in certain other relations or proportions.[1] Our main task, then, to which we must devote ourselves if our reasoning is to give precise knowledge, is so to reduce these proportions that there may emerge to our view equality between the *quaesitum* and something else already known to us. A perfect problem presents only one kind of difficulty: namely, that of so developing the proportions that they may be disentangled from the qualities in which they are enwrapped.

Now what exactly is it which, in this preparatory formulation of the problem, is being reduced to equality? We can only answer: That which is susceptible of more or less. That is magnitudes—magnitudes, in general and as such—simply *qua* exhibiting degrees, or equality, and commensurable as the two sides of an equation. This is the object of our science in so far as it

[1] Cp. *Reg. xiv*, p. 440, ll. 15-16.

is *vera mathesis* : so far as it is a rational activity of the pure intellect.

Up to this point it seems as if Descartes's criticism of the problems of the vulgar arithmetic and geometry would apply *a fortiori* to those of *vera mathesis*. A science whose sole object is the comparison of magnitudes in general, so as to make them equal or commensurate, certainly seems to be engaged in the emptiest of tasks. What could be more futile than to equate amounts of nothing in particular! But in Descartes's own account of the matter this extreme abstractness and sterility of the domain of the *vera mathesis* is corrected—or at least concealed—by the part he assigns to the imagination. He assumes that we have an imaginative knowledge of certain natures which is an indispensable condition without which the intellect cannot deduce at all. He takes for granted the sensuous or imaginative knowledge of extension, figure and motion—the fundamental characters of the physical world as we perceive it. The magnitudes in general which the intellect studies and equates are abstracted from these. They are not, therefore, amounts of nothing, for the imaginative knowledge of one or more of many and various somethings must accompany every piece of scientific thinking, though we are to pay attention only to their magnitudes. Descartes assumes, rightly or wrongly, but without question or discussion, that we can thus study or know magnitudes in general —that the differences between what they are amounts of does not at all affect the amounts. He calls in the imagination merely as an aid to the intellect in its strictly scientific study of magnitudes as such.

When we have reduced the problem to its most

perfect, abstract, mathematical formulation, we must then transfer this to real objects in extension[1] and present it to the imagination as embodied in figures so that it will be perceived by the intellect with far greater distinctness.[2] Having first extracted the abstract mathematical substance, we are then to re-embody it in one special matter—we are to make it once more an object of one special sort of imaginative apprehension.

This seems quite amazing, and seems to contradict the account given earlier of the intellect as related to sense and imagination. Is not pure intellect more precise than intellect working through the organs of sense and phantasia? One would have thought that to enwrap the purely intelligible object of science in any concrete embodiment must *ipso facto* diminish the distinctness of intellectual apprehension.

No doubt Descartes means us to replace the concrete wrapping by one of a special kind which is the object of a special sort of imaginative knowledge.[3] For nothing can be said of magnitudes in general which cannot also be applied to species of magnitudes in particular; and there is one species of embodiment most easily reproduced and depicted in imagination. That is the real extension of body abstracted from everything except its shape. This can obviously be most easily and exactly represented by the arrangement of bodily parts of the bodily organ, phantasia. Other species—differences of pitch in sound, or satura-

---

[1] *Reg.* xiv, p. 438.
[2] loc. cit.: '*ita enim longe distinctius ab intellectu percipietur*'.
[3] Cp. p. 441.

tion of colour—cannot be so easily or precisely re-produced.[1]

Nevertheless the general effect of the doctrine of the *Regulae* concerning *vera mathesis* is to attach an overwhelming importance to imagination and its picturable objects. The object of science is to reduce problems to equations of pure magnitude, but the intellect can do this only by making a preliminary abstraction from picturable, concretely embodied, magnitudes. It has to abstract amounts from natures presented to sense, in the first place; and secondly, when we have thus formed a conception of these magnitudes in general, we can do nothing with them unless we re-embody them in sensuous figures—or at least those which, for this purpose, are simplest: namely, straight lines, rectilinear and rectangular figures.[2] Descartes expressly says that throughout our abstract reasoning we must keep in our mind the concrete picturable background. We need not inquire whether it is a physical body with other properties besides the merely spatial, but we do require a body *qua* solid and shaped, and must never lose sight of it. All we require to keep clearly in mind is a spatial embodiment of the magnitudes; but we cannot dispense with that. And we must always interpret the abstracted features by reference to the concrete, picturable whole from which we have abstracted them. 'Figure' will be the pictured solid thing considered purely so far as it has shape. 'Line' will be length, not without breadth (in the sense of *excluding* breadth), but the pictured solid conceived in abstraction with reference only to its length—and

[1] Ibid.
[2] *Reg. xiv*, p. 452.

so likewise with 'point', 'plane' and the like. So also 'number' will be the object measurable by multiplicity of units. But we must never lose sight of the pictured something whose multiplicity these units express though provisionally we disregard its other properties.[1]

Descartes accuses the arithmeticians and geometers of confusion of thought. The arithmetician tends to regard numbers as abstracted from every material thing, yet as having a kind of isolable, picturable existence, whereas they are separable only as a result of his abstracting. So the geometer, having first regarded the line in abstraction as length without breadth, and the plane as area without depth, forgets that these are mere modes—abstracted features—not isolable elements of bodies. He proceeds to generate plane from line, an operation which pre-supposes that the line from which the plane flows must itself be body, whereas line proper is merely an abstracted mode of body.

Is Descartes's theory of *vera mathesis* then valueless? Rather is it the case that here he is still feeling his way and his account of it is a somewhat blundering and roundabout mixture of several different ideas. At all events, there can be no doubt about his mathematical discoveries, which he is here trying to explain, and he can be better understood by reference to those features which reappear in the *Discours*.[2] Descartes reformed the contemporary algebra by introducing an improved, easy and consistent notation, so that he was able to reformulate problems about magnitudes in terms of proportion in general. He then conceived

[1] *Reg. xiv*, pp. 442-6.
[2] Cp. Liard, op. cit., pp. 35-53.

the brilliant idea of calling geometry to the aid of algebra—calling the imagination to the aid of the intellect. Descartes's project was, accordingly, the graphic solution of equations. The third book of *La Géometrie*[1] is devoted to this task. Notwithstanding its title, however, *La Géometrie* is not geometry in the common meaning of the word, but *vera mathesis* (i.e. algebra illuminated by an appeal to spatial intuition). In the course of his work on the graphic solution of equations,[2] he was led to the discovery of the analytic or co-ordinate geometry. This is not the new universal mathematics itself, but the result obtained by reversing the procedure of the new science. The fundamental idea of the *vera mathesis* is the solution of problems expressed in algebraical terms by means of geometrical figures; but the analytical geometry is based on the idea of substituting for the spatial figure an algebraical formula which gives the law of the generation of the figure; for instance, that constituting the equation which prescribes the successive positions in a plane through which a point flows as it constitutes any required visible straight line.

Interesting as it may be, however, to observe the nature of Descartes's mathematical discovery and to find out what its relation was to his *vera mathesis*, the important question is: Does his *vera mathesis* turn the edge of the criticism threatening his method? Even the immature account given in the *Regulae* makes it clear that the *vera mathesis* assumes continunity—continuous magnitude—and assumes it is an object, not of the pure intellect, but only of the imag-

[1] Published with the *Discours* as a specimen of the new method.
[2] Cp. Liard, loc. cit.

ination. Also, the *Regulae*, more clearly than any other of Descartes's works, betrays the desperate inadequacy of his theory of the imagination, and the utter failure of the Cartesian method in explaining anything so concrete as imaginative knowledge or experience.

(i) In the first place, the method is an analysis, which proceeds by subtraction, together with a synthesis, which proceeds by addition. Therefore, a mind which reasons in accordance with this method, can deal with nothing that is not an aggregate of simples. Thus the only field of facts which it could hope to explain (without explaining away) seems to be that of numbers and numerical proportions. For everywhere else the intellect would be confronted with wholes concretely or genuinely one, unities which are not units or sums or assemblages of units. So the intellect, as Descartes conceives it, would necessarily fail to achieve knowledge, even in the spheres of the special sciences such as geometry, dynamics, physics and the sciences of life —anywhere where we come into contact with continuity, motion, and the like—and *a fortiori* in the field of philosophy.

What is here being urged against the method is precisely its abstract formulation of the principles controlling mathematical reasoning at its best; and Descartes claims to have shown that everything in the universe falls within the grasp of mathematics; except the facts, activities and achievements of self-conscious mind. But our examination shows that the chief burden of the task of mathematics falls on the imagination and not on the intellect. The intellect cannot (or at any rate does not) explain continuous magnitude, but, on the contrary, it borrows from the imagination the

95

pictured thing in order to throw light upon its own abstract procedure. Even when it is a question of discussing number, we are expressly enjoined to keep the reasoning of the intellect within the control of the imagination by reference to the concrete *res numerata*. Though he says that it is always possible to reduce (at least in part) a continuous magnitude to an aggregate, by the introduction of an assumed (fictitious) unit, this is no more than a legitimate device for facilitating measurement. But there is no evidence that Descartes thought—and he certainly does not try to prove—that the continuity of the magnitude is, by this device, explained: that is, shown to be a sum of discrete and simple units (like the postulate of an infinite juxtaposition of points in a line, which it is also convenient to suppose for certain purposes).

(ii) Secondly, the exposition in the *Regulae* brings out the defects in Descartes's account of the imagination. These are the consequences of the purely abstracting and eliminating analysis which predominates in Descartes's thought (such synthesis as he contemplates being only the adding of determinants). He applies an analysis of this kind to the contents of various forms of experience, such as sense-perception, imagination and memory, as well as of mathematical, scientific and philosophical reasoning. He detects in all an abstractly identical common feature—something to be known by a pure, undifferentiated, always identical *vis cognoscens*. So he says that one and the same power is at work in sense, imagination and reason, and that it is the instrument of knowledge in all fields of investigation. The differences which distinguish these various experiences from one another arise solely from differences in the objects to which the undifferentiated *vis cognoscens* is applied.[1] So the total experiences are not different forms of knowledge; there is only one form of knowledge: i.e. the intellect, functioning purely and alone—the *vis cognoscens* applied to ideas that are in the intellect itself. Sense and imagination are not knowledge, though they include knowledge (i.e. they include the effects of the absolutely identical functioning of the *vis cognoscens*), as one element in them. But they include, in addition, changes of states (or shape) in certain organs of the body which are the objects of this element of knowledge—or on which it casts its light. The eliminative analysis has thus reduced these apparently different modes of consciousness, each of which is a total or concrete experience, to a single undifferentiated power of knowing—a purely spiritual awareness—together with various bodily changes, to which that awareness is directed, or of which the spiritual power is aware.

It does not seem to occur to Descartes, at any rate in the *Regulae*, that any further explanation of sense-perception or imagination is required. He speaks of the *vis cognoscens* receiving shapes from the *sensus communis* or the *phantasia*; it is said to see, touch, etc. when it applies itself to common sense and imagination. So the *vis cognoscens* in imagination apprehends, in the central organ of sense, at times a sense impression (*aesthema*), and at times a *phantasma*—a survival, or record, of similar impressions apprehended in the past. In the first case it is sense-perception, in the second imagination (*phantasia*); and somehow we are able to recognize the former as the effect of an ex-

[1] Cp. *Reg. xii*, pp. 415-6.

ternal cause on the peripheral organ of sense—that is, we perceive the external thing.

Imagination here is the visualisation of certain shapes and figures in the bodily organ of imagination (*phantasia*), which is a '*vera pars corporis*', and the shapes and figures are copies of the shapes of the outer bodies. In apprehending a visual idea of a spatial figure, therefore, the *vis cognoscens* is, apparently, apprehending the shapes and mutual relations of the parts of the bodily organ of imagination, and, as this is an exact reproduction in miniature of things in the external world, we can (apparently) be confident that we are apprehending true models of the external things. But no meaning whatever can be attached to this description of sense-perception and spatial imagination, except on the assumption that the percipient knows the external causes of his imaginations (i.e. the shapes and inter-relation of parts of the outer bodies) independently of sense-perception and imagination.

But Descartes says that the *vis cognoscens* alone can know, and that it apprehends only its own ideas or changes in the bodily organ; and again[1] he speaks of imagining as a function in which we use the intellect, not in its purity, but assisted by the forms depicted in the *phantasia*. How is such a use possible on Descartes theory, unless we postulate a second *vis cognoscens* which, by employing the first *vis cognoscens* while that is apprehending the images in the *phantasia*, knows the external things?

So no results from the *vera mathesis*, and no results from his interesting theory of the physical world, can invalidate our criticism of his method. *Vera mathesis*

1 *Reg.* xiv, p. 440, l. 29f.

is not a result of the activity of pure intellect according only to the rules of the method. Yet how can it ever be 'assisted' by images? Descartes must be feeling after some more concrete form of thinking and knowing, though he fails to reach it in the *Regulae*. If he had, he would have been forced to adopt so radical a modification of his theory of method as to be tantamount to abandonment of it.

CHAPTER III

PHILOSOPHICAL ANALYSIS
OF THE CONCRETE

★

The critic who objects to Descartes's theory of the intellect and of method on the ground that the true mode of reasoning is not necessarily of this kind, will be challenged to show that any method of reasoning exists, or can be conceived, other than analysis into simples followed by synthesis into aggregates. If there is any mode of analysis which can resolve a concrete fact without disintegrating it—which can do anything other than split it up into simple natures—what is it? At least we should be able to show it at work.

This challenge raises a two-fold issue: (a) Are there any concrete facts, or wholes, of the kind alleged, that are recalcitrant to Descartes's analysis and synthesis? Is there anything in the universe, anything in the field of experience, except simples (units) and sums, links and chains? Is anything one, which is not either a simple element or a sum—a plurality of simple elements conjoined—a network of relations covering and comprehending the many, without penetrating or affecting their single natures? (b) If we assume that there really are such recalcitrant, concrete wholes—

not merely that there are objects which seem to be such because of a confusion in our limited knowledge —then in what sense, if in any, are such facts explicable or intelligible? What mode of reasoning is available to throw light upon a fact which is such that nobody, however patient he may be, could analyse it, in that sense of 'analyse' in which it means 'resolve into simple constituents that are separate and separable, from one another and from the whole; that are externally connected and separately conceived'?

As to (a), there is no doubt that we do commonly attribute a variety of modes of unity and wholeness to the objects of our experience. We do take it for granted that a many may exhibit different types of connectedness or cohesion; and also that a unity, or one of many (a complex) may differ from other unities or complexes in the kind of its one-ness, the type of its unity, wholeness or compoundedness. We shall give a general sketch of our 'ordinary' views on such matters, enumerating three main types of unity or wholeness, though some of them the plain man may repudiate and others he would not distinguish so rigidly or so dogmatically.

(i) To begin with there are wholes (though so applied the term is used vaguely) which consist of parts and are resoluble into them. Such a whole consists of parts separable from it and from one another, in existence and character, in being and intelligibility. For example, a square contains two right-angled triangles (potentially, if not actually); the number 6 consists of 3 and 2 and 1, or of six units or two 3's. Within 6, it may be said, there are the same 2 and 3 and 1 as can be conceived in isolation or may be found in some other containing number (12 or 24). In the square there are the same triangles as result from its division, or may be conceived in isolation, without ever having formed it. But these examples are open to dispute. Let us, then, take material things such as a wall or a watch. These may be taken to pieces and then put together again so as to reconstitute their respective wholes. Their various parts compose and are contained within them; but all of them may also enjoy free existence, or enter into other wholes, individually and even specifically different. Within their wholes, no doubt, the parts are related in certain ways and adjusted to one another in accordance with a certain arrangement or plan. But however essential the plan may be for the being and conceivability of the wholes, it is external to and sits loose upon the parts. The buttons of my coat are not altered whether they happen to be on the coat or off it (unless some accident disintegrates them).

(ii) In another kind of whole the relation of the parts to the whole is, at least for common opinion, in dispute: the chemical compound and its constituents. Oxygen and hydrogen do not seem to be the constituents of water in the same sense as bricks are constituents of a wall. It is true that they are isolable in so far as they can be recovered out of water by chemical analysis, but are they present in water in the same way as bricks are in the wall? Or have they been absorbed, merged into the genesis of water?

What of the principle of the conservation of matter? One may retain one's belief in that and yet deny that it is relevant to the present issue. The principle asserts that in all chemical changes something called 'matter' is not increased or diminished, but conserved;

but this something (in the case of the formation of water) is certainly not oxygen or hydrogen. It looks as though neither oxygen nor hydrogen nor yet water persists throughout the change we call combination, otherwise there would be no change or coming into being. If the oxygen and hydrogen persist, where is the change?—and the water was not there at the beginning. Still, it may be objected, this ignores what is really the important question: Is there no sense in which water may truly be said to have been, even before its perceptible emergence? What kind of modification to the constituents is necessary for a chemical change? May it not be such that they can undergo it and nevertheless persist? A scientific theory answers this question. Oxygen and hydrogen certainly are different from water, but the difference is only secondary —only in the derivative perceptual qualities—and is dependent upon persistent identity of substance. In chemical change the atoms are reshuffled; so to speak, they dance to a new tune, or are newly grouped. Water is a sort of mosaic of oxygen and hydrogen atoms with a very definite pattern, and this new arrangement is the basis of the new qualities. So the same atoms, which, moving freely in isolation, were the substantial basis of the characters we perceive in the gases, are now the basis of qualities we perceive in the water. The orthodox chemist still holds this theory, or some refinement of it in which 'equilibrium of electrical charges' (or the like) is substituted for 'atoms'.

But, even if we assume this to be true, what does the theory assert as to the relation of the chemical constituents to their compound? The atoms of hydrogen and oxygen are grouped in a determinate fashion,[1] and when so grouped they display new qualities; so the grouping has essentially altered the atoms. As grouped atoms behave quite differently, it is absurd to suggest that the grouping is a mere external arrangement. No isolated atom would dream of so behaving. Not just atoms, but grouped atoms, are the basis of the qualities of water, and it is useless to attribute these qualities, as they appear in water, to the atoms by themselves. Nor is it possible to explain the differences literally by using the antitheses of primary and secondary qualities, or substance and accident. The grouping is not analogous to the arrangement of bricks in a wall or buttons on a coat. In other words, a chemical compound differs from an aggregate in the nature of its wholeness. Here the combinables exhibit a mode of cohesion *inter se* which radically affects their existence and character.

It would be agreed that, in both of these two kinds of whole, the parts are original, primary and simple, and the wholes derivative, secondary and complex. Light is therefore, thrown on the aggregate or compound by analysis of it into its constituents and subsequent recombination. Difficulties arise, however, when one looks closely into the supposed analysis. If the aggregate were really no more than has been described above, it would not be one or whole at all. Each of its constituents is one, but no unity other than this is allowable in terms of the description given. There is no coherence of the simples; they are together, but that is how we regard them and not a way in which they *are*. So, strictly speaking, there is no

[1] Or 'pattern'?. (Ed.).

whole and the elements are not constituents; and since the aggregate is not a proper whole, it does not admit of analysis. What is called analysis is simply the picking out, one by one, of the grains of the heap. It is substituting the clear conception of many singulars for a confused and mistaken impression of wholeness.

On the other hand, it is to be noted, none of the examples given really fulfils the requirements of the description. They are not precisely and accurately aggregates in the sense required. A watch is a whole, but its wholeness is derived from the purpose embodied in it. Only as a variety subordinate to plan and as means to a common end are the 'parts' (the spring, the wheels, and so forth) parts of the watch properly so-called. But *when so considered* they are obviously not isolated nor isolable, nor are they severally intelligible, nor capable of separate existence or description. What may seem to be a mere collocation carries with it real effects in the collocated parts, which are not less real or present because difficult to trace. For example, bricks in various shapes of walls or in different positions in the wall suffer various strains and stresses; and so with pieces of wood when worked into a chair.

In the case of the chemical compound there are similar difficulties. No doubt the combinables are original and primary and the compound results from their self-sacrificing coalition. But it is, at best extremely doubtful whether the properties of the compound can be deduced from or elucidated by the properties of the combinables. Here there is scope for analysis, but could the analysis retain or explain the whole—could it throw light on its character? In the aggregate what was confused and complex was rendered, by analysis, clear and simple; but this was not really analysis, for there was strictly nothing to analyse. In the compound there is a whole to be analysed and traced back to its elements, but when this has been done we are left with the character of the compound as unintelligible as before.

However, let us ignore these difficulties here, as they usually are ignored. Let us admit that there is a character of wholeness, both in aggregates and in compounds, which the statement of them in terms of their constituents does not touch, and that 'analysis' is an inappropriate name to give the procedure which we call explaining. Still, the procedure retains a certain value. We have got things clearer by getting at the simpler elements; the constituents and combinables are conceivable definitely, and in substituting them for the wholes we do seem to have made some advance in knowledge. We learn by it—but less than we commonly suppose, and not quite that which we commonly suppose.

(iii) But there are also wholes of quite a different type the elements of which are not isolable—'concrete' wholes or concrete facts, whose parts are only constituent moments. Properly speaking, such wholes do not consist of parts and there are no isolable elements from which they are derived. Here the whole is original and substantial and the 'parts' are derivative and adjectival. The whole differentiates itself; it is not the parts which, enjoying at first each its own separate being, combine to form or are adjusted to constitute the whole. The parts are not separable even in thought—not even intelligible apart from consideration in terms of the whole. Yet, though this is so, if we wish to understand the whole we are forced to distinguish 'parts' within it and recognize them in their differences as essential to its being and to its characteristic mode of oneness.

To maintain that such wholes exist is not easy. How can we defend the notion of a whole whose parts have no character or existence except as constituting the whole? Can a whole have its unity essentially in variety? Locke cannot understand how this can be and denies its possibility (though he begs the question by admitting that it is 'made up of' its parts). To say that its unity is of the essence of its diversity, and its diversity of the essence of its unity, seems preposterous. It seems like saying that a thing is black and white all through and is each because it is the other.

Nevertheless, the kind of fact of which we are thinking is whole in one sense at least: it is genuinely single or one—not abstractly, as a unit or a simple quality, but concretely. That is, its unity, though it is continuous and is not resoluble into elements and their connections, is not a monotone. There are differences, there is articulation; and, when we reflect on what, in this sense, is a concrete whole, we must recognize in it this differentiation or diversity, and the diversity as essential to its organization or wholeness.

Although such concrete facts are, beyond question, real and though they are usually recognized, there is a marked deficiency of appropriate terminology for their description. It seems natural and easy for the mind to function (roughly) in the Cartesian manner, and in everyday life we tend to use terms which interpret wholes of this nature in Descartes's way, so long as our thought is relatively effortless and careless. The terms commonly used to mark the non-isolable 'parts' of such concrete wholes are 'features', 'aspects', 'organs', 'members'. Some, like 'aspects', are apt to suggest that the unity is really abstract and monotonous though it looks concrete and diversified; others, like 'members', 'organs', etc., tend to suggest that the parts are isolable to some extent like the constituents and combinables discussed above. Accordingly, concrete wholes of this kind may seem to be more apparent than real. But this is so, not because the parts are unreal or the wholeness imputed, but because the terms in which we describe them are unsatisfactory, or difficult, or in other respects subject to criticism. All that one can do is to select the least inappropriate of the current terms, while remembering always their inadequacy; so one may try to retain mastery of one's own terminology, and not use terms thoughtlessly so as to accept unconsciously their misleading associations.

Prima facie at any rate there are several varieties of wholes with inseparable parts. Two stand out as especially typical, but they seem to differ specifically, though further consideration might show that there are grounds for suspecting that not even these are genuinely irreducible types or species—that we are dealing here not with specifications of a genus but with variations on a theme. But we shall, in either case, find it convenient for the present to have general terms to mark the theme or genus. We shall call all such wholes 'concrete unities', and their parts—that is, any diversity of the kind that belongs to such wholes—'moments' (or 'constitutive moments').[1] We do not insist on the terms. They have been used commonly enough in some such sense in philosophy and they are not altogether inappropriate.

(a) Of the two types of concrete fact we are to consider, the first is a living organism. We tend to form different conceptions of a living organism, some less, and some more, adequate, and, therefore, likewise of its inseparable parts. We regard it as an individual whole—an equilibrium of vital activities or a concretely single cycle of such activities (the parts or moments

---

[1] The Latin word 'momentum' has (among others) the meaning of 'a decisive factor'*—e.g. the last straw breaking the camel's back. This perhaps suggests that it is an isolable constituent. Is not the last straw, an objector may ask, a separable increment to an existing burden? It is, however, only qua last that the straw breaks the camel's back, and it is only qua last that it merits the name of decisive factor, 'momentum'—that is, only as inseparably one with and completing the given burden. Given the total weight, any straw might be called 'momentum'; but no straw per se, qua isolable, deserves the title. The German word Moment is often used with the meaning required. In the analysis of involuntary movement, for instance, a German would distinguish das physiologische Moment from das psychologische Moment—two factors, each of which makes a distinct and indispensable contribution to a concrete fact, which is a change indissolubly single, bodily and psychical in one; as a curve is concave and convex at once and yet a single and indivisible direction. (Cp. Aristotle, Nicomachean Ethics, 1102 a31.) If we are to take even the first step in understanding involuntary movement, we must take into account the two 'moments', but though the distinction is in no sense arbitrary, or subjective, yet the 'moments' revealed have no separable existence, and it is misleading to speak of them as 'factors'.

* Lewis and Short give, as the second meaning of 'momentum': 'A particle sufficient to turn the scales'. (Ed.).

of the cycle are the various subordinate vital processes, such as respiration, reproduction, etc.), or else as a living and active federation of cells, or again as an immanently teleological system of co-operating organs, which in their functioning are both means and ends not only to one another but also, in a sense, to the whole.

It matters little which view we adopt, we are clearly in each case differentiating the whole, from which we start. Yet, in differentiating, we are *eo ipso* integrating it. We are not putting it together out of isolable constituents nor deriving it, by combination, from combinables in themselves separate. All subordinate activities (such as breathing, digesting, etc.) all federated colonies of cells, all co-operating organs contribute by their differences to the being and maintenance of the single, individual life—or federal unitary policy—or unitary (though far from monotonous) co-operative work. At the same time, however, these articulations, while they contribute to the whole, depend upon it for their existence and nature, their being and intelligibility. In the whole, and only in it, they live and move and have their being. Sever them in fact from the whole and they cease to be; sever them in thought, and they cannot be conceived or described adequately. On the other hand, the unity of the whole is, all the time, nothing but the conspiracy of their differences, the equilibrium of their co-operation, and its individual life is the cyclical movement of which they are the constitutive moments. Yet the inseparable organs of the living organism, though moments and not isolable parts, do seem to be, in some sense, the integrants of the whole, and so we may call them its articulations.

There are subordinate systems of activity within each system, and colonies of cells within each federation, as well as individual cells within each colony.

There is thus one typical variety of a concrete fact, of which a living organism and its articulations may be taken as a conspicuous example. This seems to be marked off from the second variety[1] because the moments of the living organism, in constituting the whole, are (or seem to be), in some sense, integrants of it, which is not the case with the other kind. If, however, you ask by whom the organism would be taken as a conspicuous example, the answer must be: An observer with some scientific education—and perhaps some philosophical education. The ordinary untrained observer commonly, not only regards as parts of the organism what are isolable (e.g. teeth), but continues so to think of them even when they are isolated. Such an observer would realize very imperfectly that, for example, an eye or a hand, which in living and functioning are genuine parts or articulations of the organism cease *eo ipso* when separated from it, to be what, by an abuse of language, they are generally called. A 'dead hand' is strictly a contradiction in terms. Though we are ready enough to speak of the organism in terms of cells, organs, and the like, we usually separate, in thought, the cells from their life, the organs from their functions and processes from the systems which carry them; and we tend to erect these abstracted organs, cells and structures into substantial things with characters which they are supposed to retain, whether the whole to which they belong is living or dead.

[1] *Vide* (b) below, pp. 112ff.

The view that such abstraction distorts the truth would probably be accepted at first by the scientist, but he would set it aside as useless for the actual detailed work of his science. He would say that we must assume the separateness of the parts for the special purposes of the science. They compel him to abstract and pay attention to the facts of the separate behaviour of the different elements and the laws which govern this behaviour. So, he would say, even in the organism, science must start from the simple and proceed to the complex, and must go on the assumption that patient investigation will detect simple constituents and discover the laws of their behaviour, whether in or out of the living whole, so that in the end we can explain the organism as a complex or composite result, as if it were an aggregate.[1]

(b) The second variety of concrete facts may be called spiritual wholes, of which knowledge (or truth), beauty (or aesthetic experience), goodness (or moral experience) are examples. The moments here are *distincta*—distinguishables into which the whole necessarily differentiates itself in philosophical analysis. Since, without such analysis, spiritual reals cannot be properly understood, the *distincta* are necessary to its intelligible being—its real or essential being. It is convenient, therefore, to call them its 'implicates'. But they have not co-operated to form it; nor do they exist

---

[1] For examples to the contrary, cp. L. von Bertalanffy, *Modern Theories of Development* (Oxford, 1933) and *Problems of Life* (London 1952); Joseph Needham, *Order and Life* (Cambridge, 1936) and J. S. Haldane, *The Philosophical Basis of Biology* (London 1931), *Organism and Environment* (Yale Univ. Press, 1917). (Ed.).

or occur, either in isolation outside it, or separably—or even inseparably—within it. Their being is no more than their emergence under that philosophical analysis which alone shows what their spiritual whole implies what in truth it is, and so what they (its moments) are. So these 'implicates', these constitutive moments of a spiritual real, are precisely what reflection on that real shows it to imply.

Here we may meet an objection. No doubt, knowledge and truth, beauty and goodness are familiar omni-present realities of human experience; no doubt they do embody and express feelings and activities of the spirit; no doubt they are feeling, will and thought realized and objective. Therefore it is reasonable to call them spiritual experiences. There really is a moral order, a kingdom of ends, sustained by and embodying the effective will for good of moral agents; and within each whole there are smaller spiritual wholes, also real —e.g. morally good institutions, and characters, and acts. And there are real aesthetic experiences, and there really is knowledge—experiences in which we possess or are possessed by truth. But there is nothing to show that these realities are the sort of wholes (with inseparable parts) that we are supposing. If they were, they could not be analysed. And if they were such wholes and could be analysed, there is nothing to show that this procedure of analysis would elucidate them or help us to understand them.

There *is* nothing to show all this, except philosophy. And, if more closely examined, the concrete facts of the first type would probably lose their apparent difference from those of the second. All such facts are the proper objects of philosophical study, with them

H

and with little else philosophy has to do. And what the philosopher does with them is to try to elucidate them by the very procedure which the above objection declares to be impossible or worthless. He analyses them, not into constituents, but into implicates. Such analysis would be, *eo ipso*, synthesis into a concrete whole which is real, because it would at once exhibit the fact constituted by the mutually implicated moments as single in a unique way, and as varied in a unique way. And since this is necessary for the discovery of the implicates, the philosophical analysis would elucidate the whole.

But there is a possible misunderstanding of the nature of implicates which must be avoided. Consider the earth's revolution round the sun. That may be resolved, mathematically, into two component movements: one in a straight line and one towards the sun's centre. Neither is actual nor a constituent of the earth's movement. Neither makes an actual contribution to the revolution. The mathematical statement does not say that they in fact co-operate to produce it, nor that they are now integrants of it, but just that the movement takes place as if it were a compromise between them. Again, the numbers 4 or 6 do not contain units, nor does the square contain lines or triangles. 3 and 1 need not, in fact, co-operate to produce 4, nor be components of the whole 4. They are reached by analysis which destroys the whole, but the whole does not contain or consist of these factors. Now it may be thought that 3 and 1 are implicates of 4; or 1, 2 and 3 implicates of 6; or two right angled triangles implicates of the square. It may be said that in such examples we have clear *distincta* with separable aspects or moments but not separable parts, and as these moments are not integrants of the whole they seem to accord with our definition of 'implicate'. But these mathematical examples fail to exemplify the proper conception of implicates in a spiritual real. For these analyses are not the only possible analyses. Each gives only one possible alternative set out of many possible sets of moments which may be distinguished by reflection on the whole. 6 may, but need not, be analysed into 2, 3 and 1; and we may suppose other sets of rectilinear figures that will together constitute a square But, in order that the moments should be true implicates, we must, for example, be able to show (a) that the earth's revolution requires precisely these and no other motions; and (b) that these motions can neither be nor be conceived except as constituting that particular motion.

It is characteristic of most philosophical theories that they are concerned with concrete facts and try to explain them by analysing them into their moments and (*eo ipso*) synthesizing them into wholes. But not all philosophers recognize expressly that such wholes are their proper subject and such analysis and synthesis their proper method. Hegel does so uniformly and consistently; Kant does so in the main, notwithstanding lapses and inconsistencies of detail. But many, who do not expressly recognize such wholes, and some who even repudiate them, are, in their actual speculations concerned with nothing else.[1] Many philosophers (especially Kant and Aristotle) will sometimes themselves profess to be seeking constituents when they are clearly looking for implicates—or what would be im-

[1] Cp. Plato, *Theaetetus* 204A, and Leibniz, *Monadology*, §§ 1-2.

plicates if their arguments were sound (e.g. Aristotle's conception of $\pi\rho\omega\tau\eta$ $\H{\upsilon}\lambda\eta$, $\epsilon\H{\iota}\delta os$ and $\sigma\tau\acute{\epsilon}\rho\eta\sigma\iota s$ as constituents of body as such).[1] Let us consider two examples:

(i) Leibniz opens the *Monaldology* with what seems to be a quite uncompromising repudiation of wholes with inseparable parts. He takes it for granted, apparently, that everything in the universe is simple or compounded of simples. A whole is an aggregate or compound with simple parts, and 'simple' means 'without parts', while, apparently, all that is not simple has parts. But the simples are 'monads', each a uniquely individual spiritual real, characterised by uniquely individual 'appetitions' and 'perceptions' which are its implicates. Its appetitions are tendencies to unroll its own series of conditions, and its perceptions are those expressions of many things in one from and to which the monad passes in its successive phases. The monad is one without parts because, unlike an extended whole, it has no isolable constituents. Yet its unity, says Leibniz, requires variety, both coexistent and successive, for it maintains its simple being in, and by virtue of its successive phases. It is a many expressed in one. It is simple concretely (that is, in and by virtue of its simultaneous internal variety); yet at each phase it is a different many expressed in one, and it maintains itself by being successive. Each monad is this and no other, because its appetitions and perceptions are these and no others—because they are uniquely graded both in their intensity and their distinctness. And they are uniquely so, because they are *this* monad's special

[1] Contrast, however, *Physics* 191a7-12, and *De Generatione et Corruptione*, 329a32-35.

phases and tendencies to change. In other words, they are its implicates—its special detail—which this monad selects out of infinitely various differences as its especial implicates. It, and it alone, is their unrolling, and at each successive phase they are its unrolling.

In a later paragraph,[1] he says that, just as a town looks different from different points of view, so the universe, though itself single, is made up of various aspects, or views of itself (i.e. monads). Each such aspect or view is the special relation to the whole of each monad in its unique and detailed perspective. This comparison, no doubt, is helpful and reliable, up to a point, and is legitimate with the reservations that Leibniz himself adds. For, strictly according to his terminology, the only reals in Leibniz's philosophy are the simple substances and their states (their perceptions and appetitions). The singleness of the universe, therefore, must be conceived as a qualitative completeness or intensive fulness of the spiritual life which is infinitely graded into the scale of monads. The infinite detail of the universe, on the other hand, is the multitudinous aspects which are the monads—the hierarchical system or articulated scale of infinitely graded monads. The total energy and life is immanent in every gradation of itself. Each monad enfolds the infinitely various detail, but each expresses or mirrors this infinite variety, this intensive fulness, which is the whole, at its own uniquely limited degree of intensity. Because every monad is thus an articulation of the total spiritual life, and because the implicates of that life constitute each in its individual degree—because that is so, therefore each change and passing condition of any

[1] *Monadology*, § 57.

one monad *eo ipso* involves a corresponding change in every other (the pre-established harmony). Hence, the self-containedness of each monad, so far from excluding, necessarily pre-supposes the adjustment of each to all.[1]

(ii) Kant's central task in *The Critique of Pure Reason* is the analysis of fact into its implicates. Fact is something essentially known or knowable by any intelligent being. That this is so necessarily implies a spiritual whole, which Kant calls 'experience' (but which might better be termed 'knowledge-or-truth'). This differentiates itself, under Kant's analysis, into two correlative articulations: (a) the self-conscious, scientific mind, and (b) its correlative, the correspondingly organized object of mind - the ordered world of physical science. Reflecting on this whole, and its two differentiations, Kant further resolves each of them into implicates. These co-implicates of both articulations of the spiritual reality, knowledge-or-truth, are the implicates of any and every fact. They appear as (e.g.) 'the manifold of sense', 'the forms of intuition', 'the schematized categories'.

If this rough sketch does represent the main drift of Kant's teaching, there is a tragic perversity in his exposition. He constantly describes implicates as though they were constituents. He talks of the forms of intuition and the categories as 'elements' of knowledge

---

[1] Cp. R. Latta, *Leibniz: The Monadology*, esp pp. 108 ff and 200-202, and B. Russell, *The Philosophy of Leibniz*, esp. Chs. XI and XII.

found in us a *priori*.[1] As a result he substitutes a description of what pretend to be stages of knowledge for the critical analysis he is plainly aiming at. He is, partly at least, responsible for the common misinterpretation of his doctrine as analysing mind into constituent parts—the various faculties—like the bits of a machine. By the same misinterpretation, the world is represented as a manifold datum, plus connections, or with arrangements, introduced into it, or superimposed on it by the mind. According to this misinterpretation, the manifold is at first passively received, and then, step by step, organized into a systematic body of knowledge by spontaneous activities of the mind (intuition, imagination, judgement, etc., in succession).

We may summarize our argument, then, as follows:

(i) The proper subjects of philosophical study are concrete facts. These are unities, but neither units nor aggregates. They are wholes, but neither complex nor compound. They are wholes with inseparable parts—wholes which determine, and are determined by, two or more implicated moments. There seem *prima facie* to be at least two more or less irreducible kinds of such facts: organic wholes with integrant parts, or differentiations and spiritual reals with implicates—wholes which imply and are implied by *distincta* that constitute but are not integrant of them. It is to be suspected, however, that, on more careful consideration, organic wholes would turn out to be disguised and imperfectly analysed examples of spiritual reals.

---

[1] *Krit. der Reinen Vernunft.* B 166. Cp. in *Prolegomena to any Future Metaphysics* § *18*, the gratuitously introduced distinction between 'judgements of sense-perception' and 'judgements of experience'.

(ii) The proper philosophical method is analysis, not into constituents, but into implicates or moments, and this is *eo ipso* synthesis. This analytic synthesis or synthetic analysis makes clear how the unity is concrete —that is, it shows the unity as an intelligible union of an intelligible variety. A two-edged process of this kind is the only adequate treatment of such matters as knowledge-or-truth, goodness and beauty—in short, any problem in philosophy: in logic, metaphysics, morals, politics or aesthetics. But the power to treat any problem thus, or to appreciate such a process of analysis, presupposes in the student a long and patient apprenticeship. The student must gradually work up to it through the lower levels of investigation, by a progress in the course of which he tests, remodels, cancels and recasts many erroneous theories of his subject.

Consider, for example, Plato's account of the origin of the state in the *Republic*, and observe the genuine and vital necessity for the earlier and imperfect analyses by which he leads up to his own mature and considered theory. Civilised society is not the result of mere contract between separate persons; not the result of selfish desires for comfort. It is not held together merely by economic necessity imposed upon separate individuals; not an aggregate of isolable constituents on which an external order is imposed. Even if it is organic, rather than spiritual, in so far as it is a whole constituted of parts, at any rate the interlocking of its parts is much more complex and vital than the relationship obtaining between the members of the 'city of pigs'.[1] The 'real' social bond, here, turns out to be the

[1] *Republic* II, 372D,

spiritual being of man in his entirety. It goes beyond economics; it is more than an adjustment of demand and supply. And society reveals itself as the co-ordination of subordinate totalities, each unique and very complicated, into a concrete whole.

Yet without the earlier, imperfect analyses, Plato's final conception could not have been formed, and it would have lacked solidity and clearness. Not only do the erroneous and imperfect suggestions throw into sharper relief the more adequate account, but this more adequate theory takes up, incorporates and transforms the elements of the preliminary and one-sided views.

And even Plato's own theory leaves much to be desired and points beyond itself to a more satisfactory conclusion. He represents the soul on the analogy rather of an organic than of a spiritual whole. The corresponding conception of the state as the soul writ large gives us the same impression. The three classes in the state (as he describes them) are (or seem to be) integrants, though indispensable and inseparable parts. His theory thus has features that are not relevant to a genuinely philosophical theory of the state, which must reveal the spiritual real—the soul with implicates as moments, and the state likewise as the soul writ large. To distinguish three classes in the state is essential to a philosophical account only if and because they are identified with certain functions and activities, not with certain groups of persons. They are moments in the life—the spiritual life—of man; not, strictly speaking, three estates, but the functions to which these correspond. Expressed precisely, therefore, the moments which Plato distinguishes are the wise administration of the laws (rather than the 'Guardians'), the courageous upholding of the laws (rather than the 'Auxiliaries'), and the conscientious producing of the necessities of life (rather than the 'artisans').

INDEX

Absolute, 66, 67ff.
Adam, C., 13, 17.
Aristotle, 32, 44f, 67, 69, 79, 83, 109, 115f.
Austin, Prof. J., 5, 82 n3, 65 n2.

Bacon, F., 55, 68.
Baillet, 16, 18, 65 nl.
Beck, Dr. L. J., 7.
Belief, 30.

Chanut, 15.
Clerselier, 15, 16.

Diophantus, 80.
Descartes, Rene *passim*.
  Discours de la Méthode, 13, 14, 51, 75, 78, 80, 82, 83, 84, 88, 93.
  La Dioptrique, 60.
  La Géometrie, 94.
  La Recherche de la Verité, 13, 16.
  Le Monde, 13, 15.
  L'Homme, 15.
  Meditationes, 13, 21.
  Principia Philosophiae, 13, 21, 32.
  Regulae ad Directionem Ingenii, passim.
Deductio, 25, 28, 31, 35, 37-48, 49, 54, 57, 59, 63, 77.

Enumeratio see Inductio.

Gilson, E., 17.
Glazemaker, 17.
Gouhier, H., 7.

Hamelin, O., 80 n1.
Heath, Sir T. L., 80 n1.
Hegel, G W. F., 115.

Illatio, 25, 27, 37ff.
Imagination (*imaginatio*), 21ff, 28ff, in *vera mathesis*, 84ff, 94, 96ff, see also *phantasia*.
Implicates, 112ff.
Imitatio, 59, 61, 88.
Inductio sive enumeratio, 38 n1. 49-61, 57.
Integrant, 110-1.
Intellect, 21, 28ff, 63, 64, 77, 94.
Intuitus, 25, 27, 28-36, 37, 49, 54, 63, 64, 77.

Kant, I., 82 n3, 115, 118-9.
Knowing, see *vis cognoscens.*
Legrand, Abbé Jean Baptiste, 15, 16.
Leibniz, G., 16, 17, 18, 115n, 116-8.
Leroy, 7.
Liard, L., 76, n1, 93 n2, 94 n2.
Locke, John, 107.